Childcraft

IN FOURTEEN VOLUMES

•

VOLUME FOURTEEN

SCIENCE AND INDUSTRY

FIELD ENTERPRISES, INC.

CHICAGO

CONTENTS

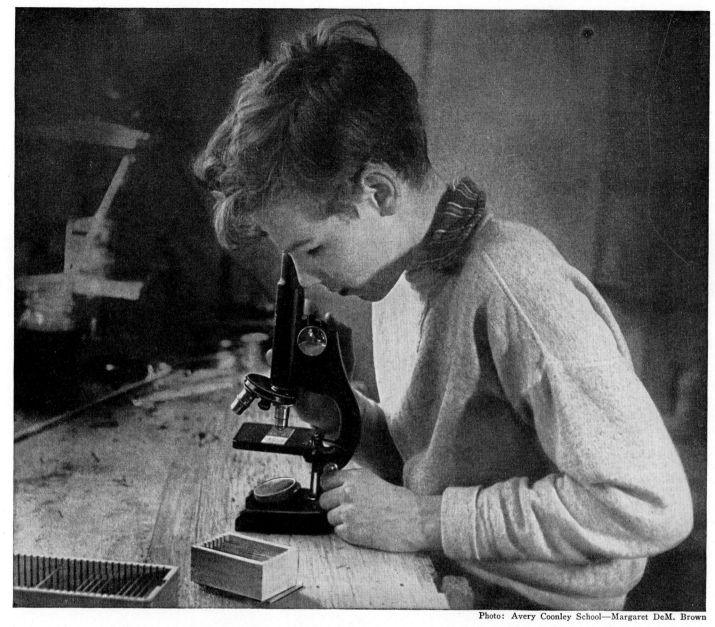

Out of a Boy's Hobby May Grow Scientific Knowledge or Even a Great Industrial Invention

INTRODUCTION TO SCIENCE SECTION

Science in its diversified aspects presents a great number of problems to children of today who are interested in physical phenomena and processes, as well as in the living things in their environment. Very young children ask science questions and they enjoy science pictures. Through pictorial representation of some of the major concepts in science, the following pages attempt to acquaint the young child with his environment and answer some of his questions.

The subject matter has been organized around certain major understandings deemed appropriate for the early elementary child. In many instances only a beginning can be made at this level. Later experiences and study will contribute further to the understandings. Parents and teachers will find much valuable material in Volumes VIII and XI on the teaching of science and on detailed descriptions of many of the living things pictured here.

Firsthand experiences are invaluable contributions toward learning and enjoying science. Consequently field excursions, home experiments, and simple constructions are recommended.

The pictures are focused on helping the child to understand seventeen major concepts as follows:

(1) Two sorts of things—living and nonliving—are found in man's environment.
(2) All living things are divided into two classes: plants and animals, of which there are many kinds.
(3) Animals and plants make more of their own kind.
(4) Some animals care for their young until they are able to care for themselves.
(5) Animals and plants change as they grow.
(6) Animals and plants are adapted to live where they do.
(7) Animals and plants are adapted to get their food in many ways.
(8) Some animals live in groups.
(9) Animals and plants protect themselves in a variety of ways.
(10) Animals and plants have different ways of getting from place to place.
(11) Some animals and plants are useful to man, while others are harmful.
(12) The earth is part of a great solar system.
(13) The neighbors of the earth influence it in many ways.
(14) The face of the earth is constantly being changed.
(15) Physical phenomena such as weather influence man's activities.
(16) Gravity, electricity, expanding steam, exploding gas, wind, and moving water are forces which help man in his work.
(17) Man has made many machines to help him use and control these forces.

In every case it is desirable that the child's interest be aroused and satisfied; that he be encouraged to remember those facts which interest him and so come into a larger understanding of the generalizations; and that he make continuous application of the facts and generalizations to his own environment.

For example: "There Are Many Kinds of Plants and Animals" presents a new idea to young children. Help them to observe some of the kinds of living things pictured here and to understand that all plants are not necessarily green and that all animals are not necessarily fur bearers. The idea that yeast, mushrooms, and other plants that are not green are really plants has never occurred to young children. They are also likely to think that mammals such as rabbits or deer are the only real animals. Insects, for example, seem to be placed in a vague classification, neither plant nor animal.

Children should come to know that every living thing is either plant or animal; that these living things vary widely in size, shape, form, and structure. That they are adapted for living and for getting food in many ways. And so on

through the ten concepts (2 to 11) that have to do with living things.

The section on nonliving things is important since it introduces the children to the forces that they encounter daily; the sun, moon, stars, which they observe; the weather, an influence on their activities; and the changing surface of the earth—something they probably do not know about.

A wide use of this physical science material will include not only careful observation of the pictures given here, but also the investigation of the environment to find similar things: different groups of stars in the sky, varied formations of frost on the windowpane. Again, a child can study forces and how they are controlled in his own home: electricity in the toaster or wind forcing the dust up into the vacuum cleaner bag.

It is not necessary that the child should understand how water crystallizes to make frost nor how resistance to electric current heats wires; it is enough that he become aware of the phenomena and forces and that he realize how many of these common things are important to him.

Space does not permit the inclusion of pictures of all nonliving or living things common to child-experience. The pictures have been selected to represent some of the most interesting phases contributing to larger science meanings. From this point it is expected that the parent and the teacher will carry the child into wider realms of scientific thinking.

Bertha Stevens, teacher of science in the Avery Coonley School, Downers Grove, helped in an advisory capacity and planned the pages on the river.

GLENN O. BLOUGH, Specialist in Elementary Science
U. S. Office of Education, Washington, D. C.

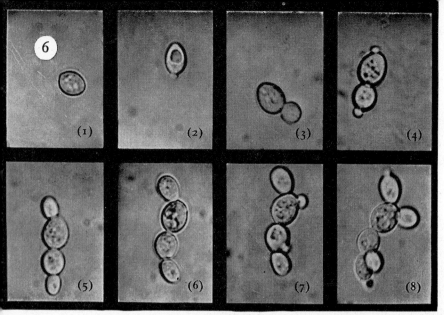

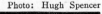

Photo: Fleischman Yeast Company

THE GROWING YEAST PLANT (above) Some plants are too small to be seen with the naked eye. Pictures (1) to (8) show yeast plants as they look under a microscope. They are not green; they have no leaves, stems, flowers, seeds, or roots. (2) Shows a tiny bud, which will grow into another yeast plant; (3) the bud after it has grown larger; (4) bud full grown with new buds formed on each yeast plant. (5) to (8) How these buds grow and new yeast plants are formed.

There Are Many Kinds of Plants

Photo: Hugh Spencer

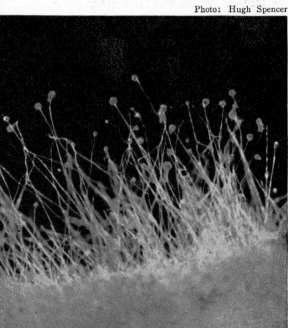

BREAD MOLD (left) Mold is another kind of plant that has no flowers, seeds, roots, stems, or leaves; it grows on bread, different kinds of fruits, and in many damp places. This mold is growing in bread. The tiny round balls are full of spores, which, like seeds, will later grow into many more plants of the same kind.

Photo: L. W. Brownell

MUSHROOMS (above) This is the "shaggy mane," one of hundreds of different kinds of fungi or mushrooms. They usually grow in damp, shady places; the shaggy mane is found in clumps in forests and pastures, and is extremely good to eat. Some mushrooms are poisonous, however, and so they should be gathered only by people who know one kind from another.

LICHEN (below) These lichens are growing on a rock; others live on stumps, trunks of trees, and brick walls. There are many different kinds, which may be gray, as this is, or black; and some even bright yellow or red.

Photo: Lynwood M. Chace

Photo: L. W. Brownell

EARTH STARS (above) These fungi are related to the giant puffball. The stars are formed when the outer skin splits and spreads as it dries. The centers are full of spores that scatter over the ground and more earth stars grow.

HAIRCAP MOSS (below) These plants grow in fields, along the road, and in the woods. Many other kinds of mosses grow on tree trunks or on the ground under trees. The tiny "caps" in the picture are full of spores.

Photo: L. W. Brownell

A ROCKWEED (right) The rockweed lives along the shore, attaching itself to rocks and growing in the salt water of the ocean. Some kinds of water plants attach their roots to the mud at the bottom of ponds and streams. Some float about in the water and do not grow in the soil at all.

Photo: L. W. Brownell

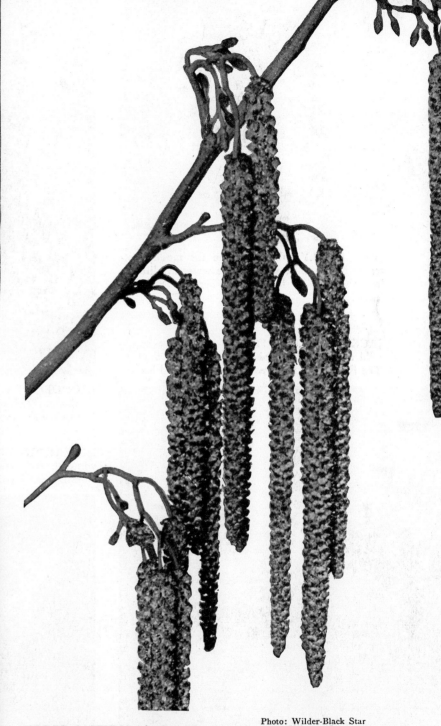

PAMPAS GRASS (below) The grasses are different from the ferns. Grasses have flowers and seeds. The stems are usually hollow, and the leaves, or blades, long and slender. There are many kinds of grasses.

Photo: Guss-Black Star

Photo: L. W. Brownell

FERNS There are many kinds of ferns and most of them grow (below) in swamps or damp woods. The spots on the fern (above) are spore cases in which develop the spores for new plants.

Photo: Topp-Monkemeyer

Photo: Wilder-Black Star

ALDER CATKINS (above) The common trees all have flowers. Sometimes the flowers are so small that they are not noticed. These are the flowers of the alder and are called catkins. (See "Trees and How They Grow," in Volume Seven.)

WATER LILY (above) From the muddy bottoms of clear, shallow water the water lily lifts its beautiful cuplike flowers and spreads its broad leaves.

Photo: Cornelia Clarke

JACK-IN-THE-PULPIT (below) A curious spring wild flower of the moist woodlands and thickets. The flowers are followed by clusters of red berries.

Photo: Hugh Spencer

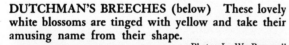

BLOODROOT (above) One of the earliest flowers to bloom. The petals are white, the center golden. Its sap is a rich orange-red, giving the flower its name.

Photo: L. W. Brownell

DUTCHMAN'S BREECHES (below) These lovely white blossoms are tinged with yellow and take their amusing name from their shape.

Photo: L. W. Brownell

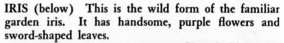

WILD ROSE (above) Whether single or double, the wild rose is beloved by children. It grows from coast to coast, and has been proposed for our national flower.

Photo: L. W. Brownell

IRIS (below) This is the wild form of the familiar garden iris. It has handsome, purple flowers and sword-shaped leaves.

Photo: L. W. Brownell

QUEEN ANNE'S LACE, OR WILD CARROT (above) It has lacy, white blossoms above gray-green leaves.

Photo: L. W. Brownell

BUTTER-AND-EGGS (below) This roadside plant has bright yellow-and-orange flowers and pale green leaves.

Photo: L. W. Brownell

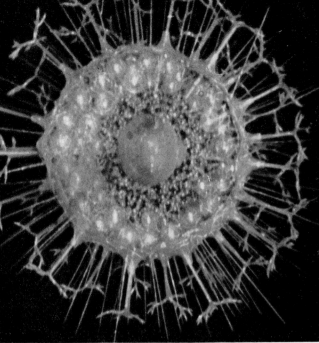

Photo: Hugh Spencer

THE SNAIL (above) Some snails live in water, and others live on land. This land snail creeps along on one foot and carries its shell house with it wherever it goes. None of the animals on pages 9 and 12 have backbones; animals without backbones frequently have shells. The feelers help the snail to know where it is going.

Photo: L. W. Brownell

THE CRAYFISH (above) The crayfish, which also lives in water, is different from all the other animals on this page: it has many legs and two long feelers; its body is covered by a hard coat, which makes a sort of armor-plating over all the soft parts of its body. The crayfish molts as it grows.

Photo: Schrage-Monkemeyer

RADIOLARIA (above) Such minute animals cannot be seen with the naked eye, but must be viewed through a microscope. Many of them live in water in aquariums, ponds, streams, and ditches.

THE SEA ANEMONE (below) One of the most colorful and beautiful of the animals without backbones is the sea anemone. Most of these flowerlike animals attach themselves to a stationary object and wait for the water currents to bring them minute plants and animals for food; others move about.

Photo: Shedd Aquarium

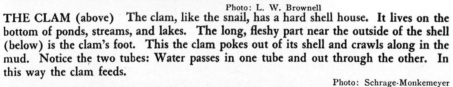

Photo: L. W. Brownell

THE CLAM (above) The clam, like the snail, has a hard shell house. It lives on the bottom of ponds, streams, and lakes. The long, fleshy part near the outside of the shell (below) is the clam's foot. This the clam pokes out of its shell and crawls along in the mud. Notice the two tubes: Water passes in one tube and out through the other. In this way the clam feeds.

Photo: Schrage-Monkemeyer

There Are Many Kinds of Animals

EARTHWORMS (below) Unlike the snail, the clam, and the crayfish, earthworms have no hard covering. They live in burrows in the ground. When heavy rain fills their burrows with water, they crawl to the surface.

Photo: Hugh Spencer

PUMPKINSEED SUNFISH

Eupomotis gibbosus

Habitat: Maine to the Great Lakes and southward east of the Alleghenies to Florida; northern portion of the Mississippi Valley; rather rare south of Virginia.

UPPER LEFT:

A pair of mated sunfishes are shown here, guarding their eggs in a shallow nest on a bare spot underwater, along the gravelly shore of a pond.

A sunfish nest is just a shallow pit made by parent fishes picking up pebbles and debris from the spot they choose, carrying such material off to the side, and dumping it. The nest-hollow is then formed and fanned clean by vigorous action of the fishes' fins.

After the eggs are laid the pair takes turns at fanning them to keep aquatic dust from settling on them and also to direct a current of aerated water flowing over them, for dust flies underwater just as it does in air and on land. Parent sunfishes guard the nest of eggs and the newly hatched fish babies from enemies of any size that they can scare or bluff. From those too large to be driven off the parents flee in dismay, fulfilling the natural law of self-preservation.

UPPER CENTER:

Here are two male sunfishes engaged in a scrimmage. Sometimes they slash away at each other with their sawlike dorsal fin spines until they damage their beautiful armor and open a way for fungus to attack their bodies. Many of their battles are of short duration, however, and largely harmless, although their spiny dorsal fins are real weapons.

A curving slash from such a fin is not to be taken lightly. When catching a sunfish, note how it sets this sharp-ended fin on edge, rolls its eyes, and struggles furiously.

UPPER RIGHT:

Sunfishes are great insect eaters. From infancy to old age, along with a host of other water creatures, they help keep the hordes of insects from completely conquering the earth. Sunfishes will eat practically anything that they can get into their rather small mouths.

LOWER LEFT:

Many kinds of fishes are able to change their colors and dusky patterns through the medium of countless color, or pigment, cells called chromatophores. These underlie the thin, transparent outer skin that covers even the hardest of scales.

Note the different patterns and colors of the fishes on this page. Except for the black bass (center figure), these are all one kind of sunfish. Those in this group show what pumpkinseeds do with their pattern when playing in a bed of tape grass, or wild celery. What a fish's eyes see in the immediate environment controls its color and pattern, through some little understood impulse. A fish placed with its head and shoulders inside a dark shelter and its tail outside will turn almost black. The eyes see darkness, so the marvelous color cells imitate darkness.

LOWER CENTER:

Here is a young sunfish playing a dangerous game of tag with an ogre of his world—the large-mouthed black bass. The sunfish is rushing away in a swift curve, at the same time paling, or turning on his invisibility colors to confuse the ravenous pursuer.

Bass and pickerel like to eat young sunfishes—grabbing and swallowing them whenever the opportunity offers. Sunfishes play about the lairs of the big fishes with little concern except at the instant of an attack.

LOWER RIGHT:

Very small sunfishes sometimes steal the angleworms from a fisherman's hook as fast as he can impale fresh worms and let them down into the water. When this occurs persistently, the fisherman can only hoist anchor and move to a spot where larger fish are more abundant than their children.

Note: The color plates of the Pumpkinseed Sunfish, the Leopard Frog, the Painted Turtle, and the Virginia Deer are by artist-naturalist Leon L. Pray, of the Chicago Museum of Natural History, who also wrote the descriptions.

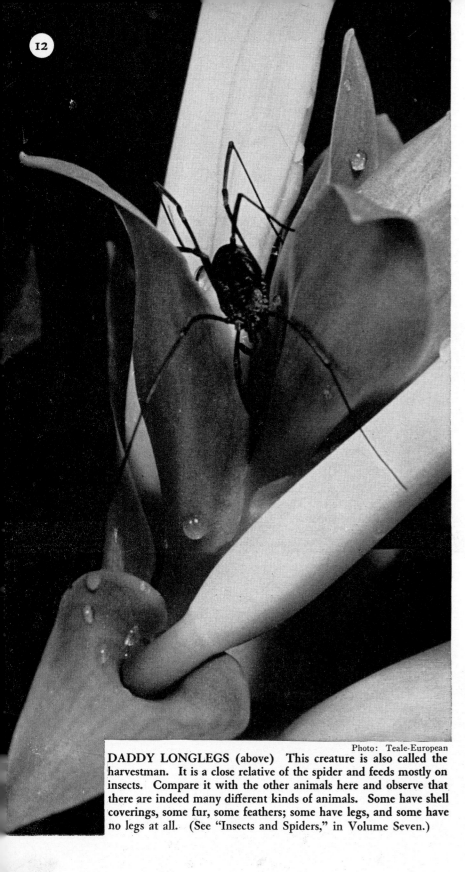

Photo: Schrage-Monkemeyer

THE LONGEST INSECT (above) The stick insects sometimes grow to be as long as nine inches; their smooth, round bodies closely resemble sticks. Many of these insects are wingless; this one, which has wings, lives in the tropics, but some stick insects live in North America. (See "Insects and Spiders," in Volume Seven.)

Photo: Ewing Galloway

THE JAPANESE BEETLE (above) The pictures on this page show some of the ways in which insects differ from each other. This one has a hard shell, as do most of the beetles. It destroys many kinds of plants, and does thousands of dollars worth of damage to crops every year.

A LUNA MOTH (below) The luna is a beautiful pale green in color. Moths, of which there are many kinds, are usually seen at night, and a bright light attracts them. There are also many kinds of butterflies, which usually fly in the daytime. Most moths have feathery feelers, while butterflies have threadlike feelers that are knobbed at the ends.

Photo: Hugh Spencer

"AN INSECT BIRD OF PARADISE" (below) This large ichneumon fly makes use of the long, threadlike parts to help lay its eggs. Insects lay their eggs in various places: some in the ground, some in cells which they make for them, some on leaves of trees. Strangely enough, certain insects even lay their eggs on other insects; when the eggs hatch, the young feed on the "host" insect. Photo: Lynwood M. Chace

Photo: Teale-European

DADDY LONGLEGS (above) This creature is also called the harvestman. It is a close relative of the spider and feeds mostly on insects. Compare it with the other animals here and observe that there are indeed many different kinds of animals. Some have shell coverings, some fur, some feathers; some have legs, and some have no legs at all. (See "Insects and Spiders," in Volume Seven.)

Photo: Shedd Aquarium

FISHES (above) The animals on this page all have backbones. They are called vertebrates. There are five kinds of backboned animals—fishes, amphibians (frogs, toads), reptiles (snakes, lizards, turtles), birds, and mammals. Fishes are different from the other animals with backbones for they usually have scales and fins. Fishes are cold-blooded. They live in water and breathe with gills. This fish is a pickerel.

Photo: Hugh Spencer

BIRDS (above) Birds are different from other backboned animals, for they have feathers. Birds are warm-blooded. There are many kinds of birds. Some, like the hummingbird, are tiny; others, like the condor, are huge. Many are fitted to swim and wade in water, others to climb on the bark of trees, and still others to live on the ground in open fields. This blue jay lives in woodlands, farms, and parks. Its nest is found in trees, often among the evergreens. (See "Our Friends of the Bird World," in Volume Seven.)

Photo: Hugh Spencer

MAMMALS Those animals called mammals are different from the other backboned animals. They have fur or hair. Mammals are warm-blooded and the mothers feed their young with milk from their bodies. They live in many different places: some in jungles, some in water, some in holes in the ground, and some climb trees. There is great variety in the food habits of mammals: some are flesh-eaters, some, plant-eaters, and still others eat both flesh and plant food. Man himself is a member of the mammal group, a flesh-and-plant eater who lives on land.

Among the many representatives of the mammals are the chipmunk (above) and the horse (below). Most of the common domestic animals, of which the horse is an example, are mammals and are described in the article "Animals That Work for Man," in Volume Seven.

AMPHIBIANS (below) Frogs, toads, and salamanders belong to a group of animals called amphibians. They live part of their life under water, part of it on land. Most amphibians have a smooth skin, and have no scales on their bodies. (See "Our Frog and Toad Helpers," Volume Seven.)

Photo: Hugh Spencer

REPTILES (below) Snakes, lizards, crocodiles, alligators, and turtles belong to a group of animals called reptiles. They are cold-blooded, are covered with scales or plates, and breathe with lungs. This is a harmless milk snake. There are many varieties of snakes; some kinds are poisonous, but only a few of these live in the United States. The rest are helpful to man, for they eat insects and destroy other harmful pests.

Photo: Hugh Spencer

Photo: Delaney-F.P.G.

LEOPARD FROG

Rana pipiens

Habitat: Northeastern and Central States

UPPER LEFT:

When spring warms the earth the leopard frog creeps from the underwater mud, where he hibernated all winter. He and his mate bulge their eyes and rub the sleep from them with their curiously humanlike hands. Before the frogs eat anything at all, they lay and fertilize their eggs in shallow, sun-warmed water along the margin of the pond or lake.

This shows the transition of a tadpole from the egg through a fishlike form to the complete young frog with tail absorbed, all ready to travel through meadow and field in search of food, including insects, especially the low-flying varieties, snails, and worms.

UPPER RIGHT:

In its meadow travels in summer the frog encounters adventure and dangers of all sorts. Snakes relish its flesh. Herons, bitterns, marsh hawks, minks, weasels, skunks—all are interested in adding frog meat to their bill of fare. The leopard frog, therefore, needs its bright, bulging eyes and its powerful, life-saving hind legs to protect it from its many enemies. With no natural weapons of defense a frog must leap for its life.

CENTER:

The curious, gluey tongue of the leopard frog acts as its "slingshot," with which it picks off insects, slugs, and snails at a short distance from its face. This pasty, white tongue can be shot forward with such speed as to puzzle an observer, who sees a frog with a fly ahead of it one second, then a faint, dizzy flash and the fly has vanished. The frog's tongue folds at the middle so that when in place in the mouth its outer end points down the throat. Creeping stealthily forward a frog can kill flies with the speed and accuracy of a rubber band in the hands of a small boy.

LOWER LEFT:

A frog can also plunge forward and seize a mouse or other small creatures too heavy for its flimsy tongue to draw in. If a blundering young field mouse should pass close by the frog, sitting still in its cranny among the meadow reeds and grass, the frog will assume a catlike role, seize the mouse by the head, with its wide mouth swiftly engulf the furry morsel and cram the reluctant and squirming hind legs in with its "hands." These members look like real hands and aid the frog in many ways at its feeding, although it cannot actually pick up objects with them. A frog's eyes shut down into the roof of its mouth; with them it squeezes large morsels of food down its throat.

LOWER RIGHT:

When not at work at the large task of filling its ravenous stomach, the leopard frog likes to bask in the sun. A lily pad out in the pond provides a lookout where it may relax and enjoy the air and warmth without worrying about predacious birds and fishes. It also likes to back into a cool pocket in the sphagnum moss, which it will shape to fit its body by curious wrigglings and contortions. Its color pattern curiously fits it to hide among coarse meadow grass and sedges. It does this when the summer sun becomes too hot for even so heat-loving a creature as a frog.

When it plunges into deep water and squirms into the mud to escape an enemy, it can remain there as long as it wishes, because its skin contains a lunglike tissue through which it takes oxygen from the water to purify its blood while its real lungs are temporarily out of use.

MIDDLE RIGHT:

At the approach of cold weather in autumn the frogs dive into the pond, squirm under the mud and rubbish in the bottom, shut their eyes tightly, and begin a deathlike sleep that lasts until the spring sun again warms the pond. Sometimes frogs congregate in considerable numbers to pass the winter in muddy bottoms of spring holes. From such retreats quantities of them are raked out by frog-hunters, to supply the market demand for frog's legs. When carried to a warm room they soon come awake and begin to sound their mating croaking as if it were really spring.

Photos: Croy-Black Star

SQUASH BUD (above) Plants that have flowers make seeds that grow into new plants. These pictures show how a squash develops.

SQUASH FLOWER (above) The bud has opened, showing the stamens, which bear pollen for the pistils, and so fertilize the eggs in the ovary of the flower. This is the part which grows and becomes the squash.

THE SWELLING SQUASH (above) The showy part of the flower has faded, and the seedcase, or squash, is beginning to grow larger. Already it has the characteristic markings of the full-grown squash.

THE RIPENED SQUASH (above) Inside this squash are many seeds. When the squash is full-grown and ripe, these seeds can be planted to make new squash plants.

WIND-BORNE POLLEN (below) Here the wind is blowing the dust, or pollen, from one chestnut flower to another, causing the cross-pollination that helps to make more vigorous seeds.

Photo: Croy-Black Star

How Plants Increase

AMERICAN LOTUS (below) At the center of the flower is the seedcase, holding many seeds. These will be borne on the water to make new plants in distant, favorable spots.

Photo: Cornelia Clarke

WILD STRAWBERRY (below) A wild strawberry can make young plants without seeds. It sends forth long, slender shoots, and new plants sprout from them.

Photo: L. W. Brownell

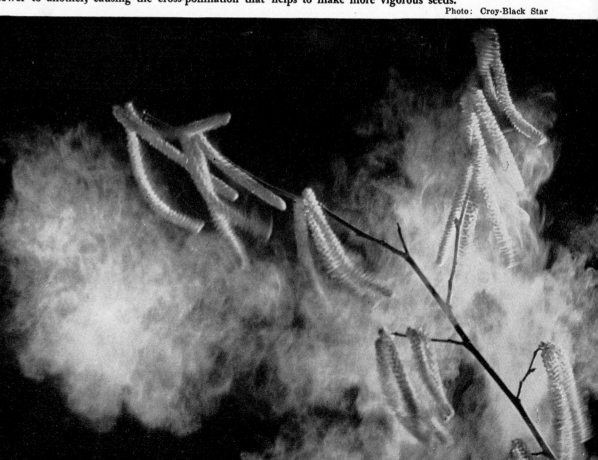

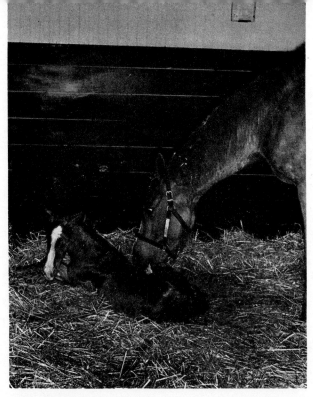

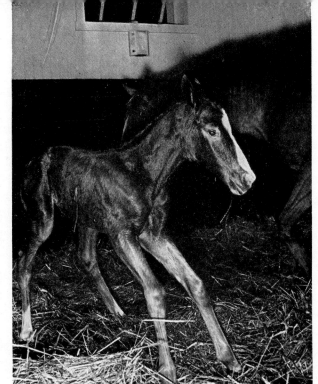

Photos: De Palma-Black Star

NEW-BORN COLT (above) Some animals are born alive, like this two-minute-old colt shown with its mother. The young of almost all mammals are born alive.

TEN MINUTES OLD (above) Some mammals are very helpless when they are first born, and some are not. This shows the colt ten minutes old; already it can lift its head; soon it will stand up.

AN HOUR LATER (above) The colt is just beginning to use its legs. At first it wobbles when it walks, but soon it will become strong enough to run and play. Note how long its legs are; they will not grow much longer.

A DAY OLD (above) The picture shows the colt in the fields with its mother. In the wild state a colt had to run at an early age.

CECROPIA MOTH LAYING EGGS (below) This moth will lay hundreds of tiny eggs, from which minute caterpillars, or larvae, will hatch. (See page 25 for stages of development of a butterfly.)

Photo: Lynwood M. Chace

MILK SNAKES HATCHING FROM EGGS (below) Some snakes lay eggs from which their young hatch, while others bear their young alive. A number of eggs in the picture have not yet hatched.

Photo: Lynwood M. Chace

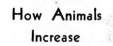

How Animals Increase

PRAIRIE CHICKENS (below) These birds make more of their own kind by laying eggs, some laying many eggs, some laying only a few. Many birds raise more than one family each year. (See page 25 for hatching chicken and its growth.)

Photo: Field Museum of Natural History

PAINTED TURTLE

Chrysemys picta, and races

Habitat: Eastern United States and west of Mississippi River

UPPER LEFT:

Here is a female painted turtle in June, busily digging her earth nest in a sandy, gravelly field far from the pond where she lives. The eggs, numbering six or eight, are well packed into the cistern-shaped nest. The mother turtle then fills in the excavated earth and scuffs the ground smooth over the spot before journeying back to the pond.

In the Northern States painted-turtle eggs normally hatch in August; laying and hatching seasons vary in different regions. At times, for some reason not well understood, the baby turtles remain within the eggshells, perfectly formed but dormant until the following spring.

CENTER, TOP:

This is a life-size drawing of the painted turtle's earth nest. The sectional view shows the "clutch" or nest of eggs, packed in sand and gravel as the mother leaves it. Below the nest is shown an egg being ripped from within during hatching by a natural cutting-point on the baby's nose. Beside this egg stands a newly hatched infant turtle, all ready to try its legs on the long journey to habitable water. Unerringly it will point its face toward the nearest water and struggle to reach its sanctuary over and through all obstacles.

Skunks dig out and eat turtles' eggs and both skunks and crows catch and eat many baby turtles before they reach the comparative safety of pond or stream.

UPPER RIGHT:

This drawing shows a battle staged by hungry painted turtles. These usually slow-moving animals, with their mild, almost humorous, little striped eyes can put up a spunky fight when stirred to action by jealousy over a bit of food. The small gladiators here are snapping and tearing away at each other's tough hides, fighting for a dead fish. When their breath gives out, they let loose and rush to the water's surface, to blow and gulp lungfuls of fresh air, only to remember their dispute and paddle swiftly down, renewing the scrimmage. At times several other turtles are attracted to the spot and join wholeheartedly in a free-for-all, while some sly one among them may steal away with the booty.

LOWER LEFT:

A peaceful, underwater view of turtles leisurely picking up a snack of water insects, which form a large part of their food. In midsummer when near a pond where there are turtles, listen for a sharp, smacking sound among the lily and spatterdock leaves. This is caused mostly by turtles snapping insects and snails from the edges of lily pads.

The small species of turtles in our lakes and ponds play a useful part in keeping down the number of insects of both land and water.

LOWER CENTER:

Here the turtles are seen at their favorite outdoor sport, lazily basking on a waterlogged tree trunk. With full stomachs and drowsy heads, they like to clamber out of water into a safe place where the breezes play over them and the sun warms their backs.

Some are always on the alert; and if an enemy approaches from air, land, or water's surface, they all tumble off the log and dive into weeds or mud to hide until the danger is past.

LOWER RIGHT:

Winter finds the turtles snug and cosy where they have dug themselves into the mud and debris at the bottom of some quiet cove of the pond, there to sleep the cold months through.

In the springtime hosts of turtles may be seen where they have emerged from a massed winter gathering. At sight of a person the turtles will start a concerted rush for deeper water, making a noise like an avalanche of cobblestones as they disappear beneath the surface.

KINGFISHER AND FLEDGLINGS A kingfisher (left) is bringing food to its hungry young (right). The young were hatched in the bank of a stream in a nest lined with the bones of fish. At first the young were helpless. Here the fledglings have come out of the nest, but they still cannot catch their own food, and must be fed by the parent birds.

Photo: Ewing Galloway

Photo: L. W. Brownell

Some Animals Care for Their Young As They Grow

SWANS AND CYGNETS (below) The young swans, or cygnets, stay with the adults for many months after they are hatched. The swans keep watch over their young, and protect them against enemies. Some young birds, like the killdeer, need very little care; they leave their nest soon after they are hatched, and find their own food.

Photo: Hibbs-European

NEST AND EGGS OF THE CANADA GOOSE (below) The goose has lined the nest with down, which she pulled from her breast. When she leaves the nest to get food she covers the eggs with the down to keep them from getting chilled. After the young have hatched she feeds them, but they are soon able to walk and swim.

Photo: Lynwood M. Chace

EAGLE BRINGING FOOD FOR ITS YOUNG (below) Some animals, like the frog and turtle, do not take care of their young at all. Many other kinds of animals care for their young for a long time after they are born. Eaglets are helpless and remain in the nest for several weeks.

Photo: Field Museum of Natural History

Photo: Dunton-New York Aquarium

A NEST-BUILDING FISH (above) Most fish do not take care of their young, but a few do build nests. This stickleback is working on its nest, usually made of twisted stems glued together by the fish. The male guards the nest.

Photo: Field Museum of Natural History

SEALS WITH THEIR PUPS (above) Seals live most of the year in the sea, but always clamber onto the rocks along the shores to have their young. They live together after the pups are grown.

RACCOON (below) This mother raccoon is carrying her baby to a place of safety by the scruff of the neck. She cares for her young for a year, sometimes longer, until they can look out for themselves.

Photo: Lynwood M. Chace

Photo: Lynwood M. Chace

THE CARPENTER ANT (above) These ants live in runways in dead tree trunks. The white objects are cocoons in which new ants develop. If nests are disturbed ants scurry about carrying eggs, larvae, and cocoons to a place of safety. (See "Insects and Spiders," in Volume Seven.)

WASPS These insects also care for their young. The queen lays the eggs, the workers care for and feed the larvae. Here is a worker (1), a male (2), and a queen (3). The picture of a wasp nest (below) shows where the young develop.

Photos: Palmer-Black Star

Photo: Souris Grise-Black Star

KANGAROO (above) The baby rides in the mother's pouch.

OPOSSUM (below) The young also are carried in a pouch and when older ride on the mother's back.

Photo: Field Museum of Natural History

VIRGINIA DEER

Odocoileus virginianus

Habitat: Virginia, Pennsylvania, and New York. Type locality is Virginia. (Under name of whitetail, including known races, the habitat covers eastern United States, watercourses of Great Plains, southeastern Canada, some territory in southwestern United States and northern Mexico.)

———

UPPER LEFT:

In the United States the Virginia, or white-tailed, deer give birth to their young in May or June. The period of gestation is approximately seven months. The fawns are beautifully spotted with white on a brownish body color. This pattern looks like flecks of sunshine falling through overhead leaves upon a carpet of last fall's leaves and so helps to conceal the fawn when the mother wanders away to graze.

Young fawns are as playful as puppies or kittens. They leap about, stand erect, and spar with their swift moving forefeet. They hold long head-butting contests and pushing melees, which strengthen their muscles and sinews to stand them in good stead for racing away from danger or fighting adversaries when they grow to maturity. Healthy deer are slender but extremely powerful. A big man's strength is as nothing when pitted against that of even a young buck deer in autumn.

UPPER CENTER:

The series of three male heads shows the development of antlers at different ages up to "prime." The left-hand head shows a buck in the autumn of his second year. He may have two points on each antler, but usually only one. The center head shows him at three years. He may have many or few points on his antlers, but the antlers are usually small. The right-hand head is of a four-year-old buck with full swelled neck in autumn and a fine set of antlers on his forehead. They may have a few or many points as in the preceding year. As the male grows older, if he remains healthy and vigorous, his antlers will become heavier and more burly at the base. In old age his antlers will be poor in shape and weak in inner structure.

UPPER RIGHT:

The Virginia deer's constant nightmare is the great, gray timber wolf (inset), which travels in a pack. Wolves may raid a winter deer "yard," killing all the helpless animals in one raid. In summer wolves often hunt singly, skulking through the silent forest. It is a fearsome experience to hear the sudden outcry of a young fawn in the night, followed by the maddened plunging and bleating of the mother deer when a lone wolf has seized the fawn.

Deer seek cool lakes and streams in summer where they feed on succulent water plants and sink their thin bodies in the water and mud out of reach of biting insects.

During the time that the summer coat of red hair is growing (about two and one half months), the new antlers attain their full size. While growing, the antlers are pulpy at the outer ends, club-shaped, entirely nourished by arteries and veins, and furnished with exceedingly sensitive nerves throughout their surface, which is covered with tough skin and a coat of fine fur, unlike the hair which covers the body.

CENTER:

In the North the mating season comes in October and November; in the South in late November and December. Then the lean, red-coated appearance gives place to a fat, sleek, brownish-gray exterior, with the antlers of the bucks hardened and cleared of their covering of "velvet" by thrashing about in the brush and weeds.

When first uncovered, the antlers have the color of freshly-dried bone; but usually before the velvet has all been stripped from them, a rich, brown stain begins to accumulate from the tannic acid of brushwood, bark, and leaves, against which the deer thrashes to clean off the ripe velvet. The antler points are sharpened and polished by being jammed repeatedly into the earth. A mating male deer is one of the most alive and wildly animated figures imaginable. He begins his pursuit of consorts with a prime layer of fat upon his ribs. He scarcely eats at all, but rushes about between spells of resting, seeking love and battle, so that at the end of the mating season he is little more than a shivering rack of bones covered with a dishevelled, though cold-resisting, coat of hair. When his fever has calmed, he begins to feed ravenously; and by the time the cold of real winter arrives, he again has a layer of fat upon his frame, so that he may enter the season of scanty fare in comfort.

LOWER LEFT:

With the arrival of deep winter snows in the North, deer seek browse, moss, and lichens to supply their needs in food. As snow piles deeper and deeper, the deer herd together and trample out more or less intricate yards of crossing and recrossing paths, through which they move in quest of food.

LOWER RIGHT CENTER:

Toward spring the antlers of male deer loosen from the skull and soon fall to the ground to become food for hard-toothed deer mice and porcupines. On the forehead of a buck at this time are left two small, more or less blood-stained, bare spots of exposed bone. Over these bare-topped, bony knobs the surrounding skin begins to expand, slowly covering and healing them, like new bark growing over the scar of a sawed-off tree branch.

While the deer's winter coat remains prime these bare, skinned-over spots are dormant, waiting for the thrust of springtime to stir them into growing activity.

LOWER RIGHT:

As spring warms the earth the heavy winter coat of the deer begins to loosen and is soon shed, to be replaced by the beautiful red garb of summer. As soon as new hair begins to form in the skin, the dormant antler-seats upon the buck's forehead spring into life. The skin over them commences to bulge; becomes tight and shiny. Then, as the new coat appears on the body, an amazing thing takes place: A thick, furry knob buds upward from each antler-seat. These swelling buds are the beginnings of the great battle weapons that are to decorate the proud crest of the warrior of the scarlet and gold forests of autumn.

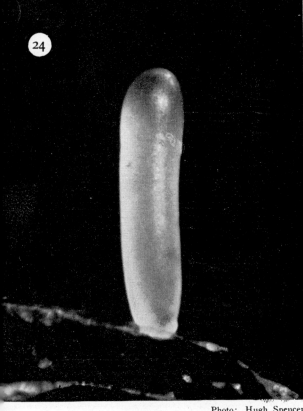

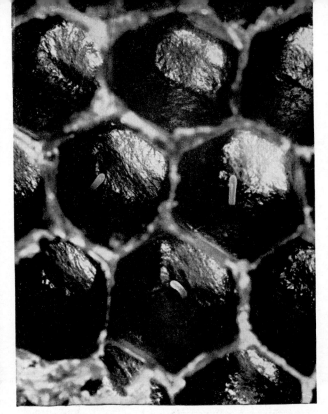

Photo: Hugh Spencer

EGG OF BEE (above) The queen lays an egg in each cell.

EGGS IN CELLS (above) The tiny, white objects are the eggs, which hatch into grubs, or larvae.

GRUBS IN CELLS (above) These wormlike grubs are fed by workers, shed their skins, and become pupae.

Photos (except upper left): Croy-Black Star

A GRUB (above) The workers build the wax cells and fill them with food for the grubs.

PUPA (below) This is a quiescent time, during which it becomes an adult bee.

FULLY FORMED BEE (below) This picture shows a bee, now fully formed, which has been removed from the cell just before it was ready to emerge.

A NEW BEE EMERGES (below) The bee is now pushing its way out of the cell. It will soon be ready to begin its work in the hive.

DRYING ITS WINGS (below) Soon this bee will be lost among the thousands of others of the swarm.

(5)

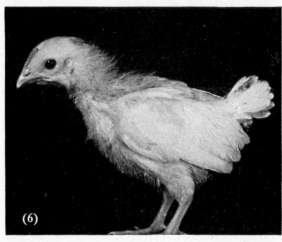
(6)

(7)

(8)

Photos. W F Lamoreux, Department of Poultry Husbandry, Cornell University

THE DEVELOPMENT OF A CHICKEN (above) With innumerable pecks, the chick makes the first break in its shell; an hour later this wide crack begins to show the chick inside (1); four hours after the pecking begins the crack completely encircles the shell (2); forty minutes later the chick is able to push its way entirely out of the shell (3) and (4). That same day the chick can run about (5). Its down has now become dry and fluffy. In eighteen days (6) the chick's feathers are well developed, especially the wing feathers; (7) the full-grown bird that laid the egg in which the chick developed. Young hens, or pullets, lay eggs when about six or seven months old. This rooster (8) was mated with the hen above, and is the father of the chick that hatched from the egg.

Photos (lower half page): Hugh Spencer

MOSQUITO (left) Mosquitoes change in appearance as they develop from eggs, which hatch into larvae, or wigglers (1). These live in the water and gradually change to pupae (2). Finally the pupae come to rest at the surface of the water, and the adult mosquito (3) emerges, a process which may often be observed in stagnant water.

THE BLACK SWALLOWTAIL (below) The egg (1) laid on a plant that will provide food for the larvae. The caterpillar, or larva (2), hatches from the egg. It eats, molts, and grows. Finally the larva makes a chrysalis around itself and inside takes on the pupal form, which later becomes an adult butterfly. A swallowtail (4) has now emerged from the chrysalis. The female lays eggs, and the cycle begins again.

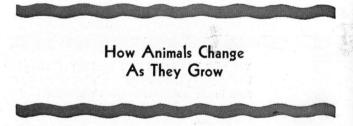
(1)

How Animals Change As They Grow

(1)

(2)

(3)

(2)

(3)

(4)

Photo: Cornelia Clarke

A BLOSSOMING CACTUS (above) Their extraordinary drought resistance makes cacti the most famous of desert plants. They are often cultivated for their showy flowers.

Plants Are Adapted To Grow Where They Do

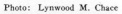

WATER HYACINTHS (below) This plant with its enlarged parts containing air is especially adapted to float in the water. The roots take their food material directly from the water and do not grow in the soil at the bottom.

Photo: Lynwood M. Chace

Photo: Ewing Galloway

DESERT FLOWERS (above) Some desert plants send their roots far down to get water, others have a shallow root system which utilizes even a light rain.

MOUNTAIN FLOWERS (below) Growing at high altitudes where nights are cold and where snow falls most of the year. This avalanche lily grows quickly and is short-lived. It pushes through the snow to blossom in the warmth of the sun.

Photo: Ewing Galloway

Photo: Steiner-Black Star

EARLY SPRING FLOWERS (above) Many early spring flowers blossom even before the snow has melted and long before the forest shade of summer shuts out the sun. The buds were formed in the previous autumn and food is stored in the roots. The first warmth of spring melts the snow, water enters the roots, and growth begins.

SAND DUNES (below) Shifting sand of the dunes often covers plants and chokes them. These grasses have broad-spreading roots to hold the sand when the wind blows, and hairy stems and leaves to hold moisture.

Photo: Barry-Black Star

Photo: European

POLAR BEARS (above)   Fat and white, thick fur are adaptations which fit the polar bear to exist in the coldest regions.   Polar bears are excellent swimmers and have been seen a great many miles from land.   They are hunters of seal and fish.

GREAT HORNED OWL (below)   An owl's eyes are adapted for seeing in dim light; it has soft feathers on its wings for silent flying, and a sharp beak and claws for capturing food.   Its mottled feathers blend into the night shadows, making it almost invisible.

Photo: Harold M. Lambert

Animals Are Adapted To Live Where They Do

GILA MONSTER (below)   This large, desert lizard, the only poisonous one in the United States, has a tough, scaly skin as protection against the loss of body moisture.   It can live for a long time without eating, while the tail, which stores fat, grows steadily smaller.

Photo: L. W. Brownell

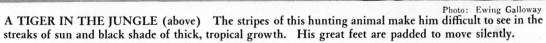
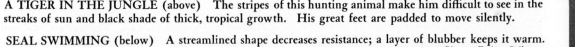

Photo: Ewing Galloway

A TIGER IN THE JUNGLE (above)   The stripes of this hunting animal make him difficult to see in the streaks of sun and black shade of thick, tropical growth.   His great feet are padded to move silently.

SEAL SWIMMING (below)   A streamlined shape decreases resistance; a layer of blubber keeps it warm.

Photo: Ewing Galloway

Photo: Cornelia Clarke

A BUILDER (above) The muskrat lives in marshlands, where it constructs a dwelling from reeds and mud. Adapted for water living, it is a good swimmer with webbed hind feet. Its teeth can chew hard foods.

A WADER (below) The pelican's webbed feet keep it from sinking into the oozy mud. The beak is made for catching fish; the pouch stretches to hold water.

Photo: Jacobi-Monkemeyer

Photo: Hagenbeck-Monkemeyer

A LEAPER (above) These mountain animals, with their strong legs and sure hoofs, are adapted to leaping over rough, rocky surfaces.

A SWIMMER (below) The sea turtle's shell serves to buoy the weight upward, although some specimens weigh as much as a thousand pounds. The feet are modified to push against the water.

Photo: H. Armstrong Roberts

Photo: Lynwood M. Chace

A CLIMBER (above) This baby squirrel is well adapted to climb trees. Although its eyes are not yet open, already its sharp claws can cling to the bark. Its color resembles that of the bark. In a few weeks it will leap from branch to branch, using its tail as a rudder and balance. Its sharp teeth can open nuts.

Photo: Croy-Black Star

AN INSECT HUNTER (above) Insects have different ways of getting food. Some fly; some find food in the ground or under the bark of trees; others get it from leaves, stems, and roots of plants. Some lay eggs in the bodies of other insects and these will become food for their young. This insect feeds on other insects.

Photo: Harold M. Lambert

ELK IN WINTER (above) This elk, or wapiti, has scraped away the snow and found moss and grass to eat. Sometimes elk eat the tender bark of trees, or the leaves from the lowest branches.

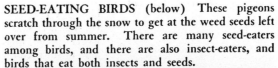

SEED-EATING BIRDS (below) These pigeons scratch through the snow to get at the weed seeds left over from summer. There are many seed-eaters among birds, and there are also insect-eaters, and birds that eat both insects and seeds.

Photo: Schaub-F.P.G.

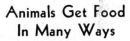

Animals Get Food
In Many Ways

THE OTTER (below) The otter could never get its food in the same way as the elk does. Its webbed feet and its tail make it possible for it to swim through the water to catch fish for food.

Photo: Ewing Galloway

Photo: Lynwood M. Chace

A FLESH-EATING BIRD (above) Eagles, hawks, and owls are a few of the flesh-eating birds. Here is a hawk using its sharp beak and claws to tear at its food. Its sharp eyes can detect a mouse from hundreds of feet in the air, and it drops swiftly. Hawks are said to fly at a speed of almost eighty miles per hour. (See "Our Friends of the Bird World," in Volume Seven.)

Photo: Lynwood M. Chace

HAWK MOTH'S TONGUE (above) The moth could never eat the kind of food the insect hunter eats, for its long tongue, kept folded up like a watch spring, is made to unroll and sip nectar from flowers. Observe on these two pages how many different ways animals get their food. Can you think of any more?

PRAYING MANTIS (below) This fierce-looking creature eats caterpillars, grasshoppers, and many other insects. Its powerful front legs are especially fitted to grasp its prey and hold on until it has finished its dinner.

Photo: Scofield-Black Star

Photo: Teale-European

THE HONEYBEE (above) The short tongue of the honeybee is satisfactory for most flowers, but it is unable to lap up nectar from the honeysuckle and red clover. A larger species, the bumblebee, with its long tongue, is easily able to sip nectar from the clover.

AN ANTEATER (below) This animal has no teeth, but a long, sticky tongue, which it thrusts into an anthill and laps up the ants. An anteater could never eat the kind of food the hawk preys upon, nor the kind the squirrel eats. Not only the food-eating parts of animals but also their swift wings, their soft-padded feet, their long claws, or even their protective coloring, are adapted for food-getting.

Photo: Bridges-New York Zoological Society

Photo: De Palma-Black Star

A TURTLE AT LUNCH (above) Turtles have no teeth, but they have strong jaws with sharp cutting edges. Some, like this one, live in water, and get their food there. Others live on land. Sea turtles have flipperlike legs and can swim to catch their food.

THE SQUIRREL (below) Rodents are sharp-toothed animals that eat nuts and other hard foods; their teeth are so made that they can gnaw through the shells of nuts or the bark of trees to get at the edible parts inside. Not only squirrels, but rats, mice, rabbits, beavers, muskrats, and porcupines are classed as rodents, and they all eat similar foods.

Photo: Monte-European

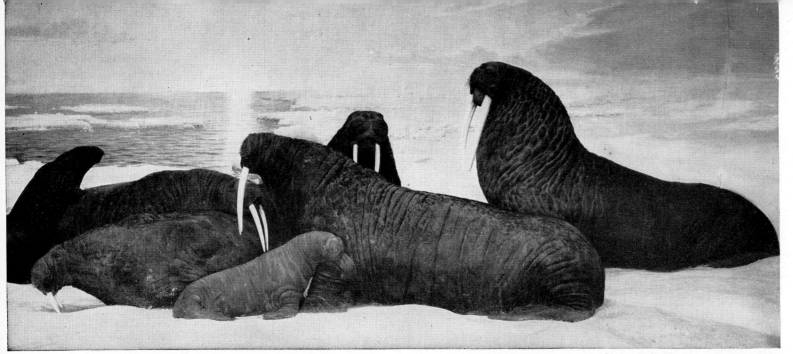

Photo: Field Museum of Natural History

WALRUSES (above) These animals are usually found in small herds of a dozen or so. The walrus is at home in water but is awkward on land. It is harmless if let alone, but if one of a herd is attacked, all the others will come to defend it.

A BEAVER COLONY (above) Some animals live together in groups. Here are beavers cutting trees. There are two beaver houses; one is on the shore at the right, the other is in the pond. The beaver dam at the left holds back the stream to make the pond in which beavers get their food, swim and play together.

A SMALL HERD OF BISON (below) The bison, or American buffalo, usually lives in a herd. Before so many of them were killed, there were great herds of thousands on the plains of the West, quite safe from every enemy but man. So many buffaloes have been killed that only a few are left in National Parks, where they are protected and fed by men in the cold winter when food is scarce.

Photo: Lajtha-Black Star

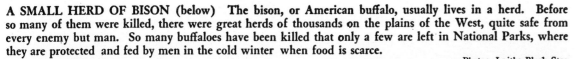

Some Animals Live In Groups

SWALLOWS AND THEIR HOMES (below) These nests are built of mud on the side of a barn. Sometimes swallows build their homes in mud or sand banks. Birds seldom live together in colonies as swallows do; and usually they live in families only while rearing the young.

Photos: Field Museum of Natural History

BEES AND THEIR QUEEN (above) Certain kinds of bees, ants, and wasps live in swarms. These honeybees divide the work of the hive, some gathering food, some guarding the hive, others cleaning the hive or doing various work. The queen lays the eggs and is the mother of the swarm. The white arrow indicates the queen.

Photo: Croy-Black Star

Photo: H. Armstrong Roberts

A FLOCK OF GANNETS (above) These birds nest together in great flocks as seen here. Among the thousands of seaweed nests, each bird knows its own pale-blue egg, and flies directly to it, although there may be another bird's egg only a few inches away. Here the young birds are hatched.

A HERD OF ELK (below) Elk live in herds as the buffaloes do. Once they were abundant in many parts of the United States. Now most of them live in small herds in Wyoming, mainly in and around Yellowstone National Park. Usually elk spend the summer high up in the mountains, and in winter come to lower lands where they can find food.

Photo: Korth-Black Star

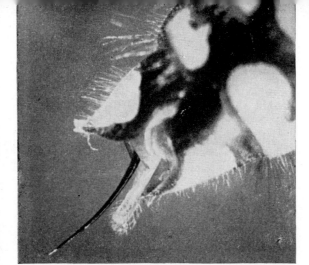

Photo: Lynwood M. Chace

THE HORNET'S STING (above) The sting, at the lower end of the abdomen, is stabbed into its victim, and a poison is injected under the skin to cause pain in large creatures, and paralysis and death in small victims. Bumblebees, honeybees, wasps, and some other kinds of insects protect themselves with stings similar to this one.

Photo: De Palma-Black Star

THE ARMADILLO'S ARMOR (above) Protection from many of its enemies. The shell has many overlapping hard plates, covering not only the body, but also the head, feet, and tail. When an armadillo is disturbed it rolls itself into a hard-shelled ball so that the softer parts are protected. These animals are most often seen at night, feeding on insects dug from the ground.

Photo: L. W. Brownell

THE RATTLESNAKE'S FANGS (above) It is easy to see how this poisonous rattlesnake protects itself. The sound of its rattles warns enemies to keep away for the poison from its fangs will kill them. It is the color of the ground, and thus escapes notice when hunting or hunted.

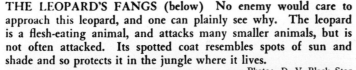

THE PORCUPINE'S QUILLS (below) The sharp, barbed quills stuck into the flesh of an enemy cause great pain. At the approach of danger a porcupine lowers its head, arches its back, and rolls into a ball. The porcupine cannot shoot its quills as some people believe, but the quills are loose and come out easily.

Photo: Krainin-Black Star

THE LEOPARD'S FANGS (below) No enemy would care to approach this leopard, and one can plainly see why. The leopard is a flesh-eating animal, and attacks many smaller animals, but is not often attacked. Its spotted coat resembles spots of sun and shade and so protects it in the jungle where it lives.

Photo: D. V. Black Star

How Animals Protect Themselves

HERMIT CRAB'S SHELL HOUSE (below) This crab is sometimes found in burrows, but more often it backs into the deserted shell of another sea dweller. The hinder parts are soft, and the shell protects the crab from becoming food for other animals.

Photo: L. W. Brownell

A SHELL (above) The turtle can draw its head, tail, and legs into its shell and there be safe from harm; it resembles the soil over which the turtle crawls. Some turtles look so much like stones that they are never noticed. What other animals on these pages protect themselves by means of a hard covering?

Photo: European

A LEAP (above) If frightened, the kangaroo can leap as high as seven feet. The long hind legs enable it to leap away from its enemies to safety. Many other animals like the deer and the antelope escape from their enemies by means of their strong legs and swift running.

Photo: Ewing Galloway

Photo: Hugh Spencer

AN ODOR (above) When a skunk is disturbed, it gives off such an unpleasant odor that its enemy quickly disappears. A few other animals also produce odors, but none so offensive as the skunk's.

Photo: Ewing Galloway

A TOUGH HIDE (above) The alligator looks like its surroundings, and could easily be taken for a log. Its mighty jaws and sharp teeth also protect it.

ANOTHER SHELL (below) This is a snail gradually emerging from its shell and beginning to move about. The snail can quickly draw its head and other softer parts back into the shell if there is danger. Note the smooth pad, or disk, which tightly seals the creature inside. See how cautiously it emerges, a fraction of an inch at a time, after whatever disturbed it has gone.

Photos: European

Photo: L. W. Brownell

Photo: Lynwood M. Chace

Photo: Krause-Black Star

THE TOAD (above) One must look closely at the pictures on this page to find the animals. They have all taken on the coloring or patterns of the places where they live. A toad looks like the ground on which it squats. Some toads can match the colors of the places where they are, changing from the green of vegetation to the brown or gray of soil.

TWIN FAWNS (above) The spotted sides of the young of the deer look much like the ground with sunlight filtering on it through the branches of trees. Before the deer are full grown the spots disappear. Their great speed then becomes their chief protection. (See color plate on page 23.)

SPHINX MOTHS (above) They resemble the gray bark of trees and are almost invisible. Often the underwings, brightly colored, can be seen only when the animal flies or spreads its wings.

THE WILD DUCK (below) The mother is not noticeable on her eggs among the leaves and grasses. Her feathers look much like twigs and dead grasses, as she sits so quietly. An enemy might pass close to her and never see her there at all. Her babies will hide in the same way.

Photo: Ewing Galloway

THE SNOWSHOE RABBIT (below) In winter this rabbit turns white to look like the snow and so escapes notice. In summer it changes to a grayish-brown color. The weasel is another animal that changes the color of its coat.

Photo: Korth-Black Star

A DRAGONFLY (above) Animals have many ways of getting from place to place. This dragonfly darts swiftly over water on its delicate wings.

Photo: Teale-European

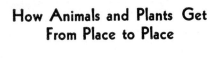

How Animals and Plants Get From Place to Place

A SEA GULL (below) This bird is well fitted to move through the air, for its strong wings carry it great distances. Gulls can swim, too, with their webbed feet.

Photo: European

BEARS (above) These bears are good climbers with their muscular limbs and sharp claws. Though many small animals climb in search of food or to escape enemies, only a few of the larger ones can climb trees. A bear shuffles quickly out of sight on the ground.

Photo: European

Photo: Mayer Black Star

AN OPOSSUM (above) This creature climbs in search of food, wrapping its tail around the branch and hanging on while it eats or reaches for food.

STARFISH (below) These are not real fishes, for they do not have backbones or fins. Here they are clinging to the glass of an aquarium with tiny "tube feet," or suckers, which enable them to move about.

Photo: Croy-Black Star

THE HAIRY WOODPECKER (below) has sharp-clawed feet and a stiff tail to help it climb.

Photo: Field Museum of Natural History

THE REPTILE SKELETON

Photos: Bridges-New York Zoological Society; and Schrage-Monkemeyer

A BOA CONSTRICTOR (above) Like other snakes, a constrictor moves by using the scaly plates on its undersurface. These are attached to the muscles of the body, and these muscles to the ribs. The skeleton of a python (below) shows the backbone and ribs that help the snake to move.

A BAT (below) These are not birds. They have no feathers; instead they are covered with fur, and they feed their young with milk as do all mammals. Bats stay in such dark places as caves and barn lofts during the day, and come out in the evening to catch insects. They fly through the air on swift, silent wings, catching mosquitoes and other insects harmful to man. They are no more likely to fly into a person's hair than birds are.

Photo: Cornelia Clarke

Photo: Allara-Black Star

A SALMON (above) Fishes sometimes move so swiftly through the water that they can scarcely be seen. This salmon is traveling up a river, leaping over the falls. It will try and try again until it succeeds, and then will continue its journey upstream. With an unfailing instinct salmon always return in the mating season to the river in which they were hatched.

A MOLE (right) When burrowing through the ground and traveling about in the tunnels it has built, the mole's front feet are like strong shovels for they help it to dig and crawl about underground.

Photo: Cornelia Clarke

A FLYING SQUIRREL (below) This squirrel leaps rather than flies. It spreads the membranes between its body and its legs, and parachutes down from high places.

Photo: L. W. Brownell

Photo: Hugh Spencer

MILKWEED SEEDS (above) Plants, like animals, often travel. The whole plant cannot fly, but the seeds can, and each seed has a tiny plant inside.

COCKLEBURS (below) These seeds "hitchhike" to far places by catching on to fur-bearing animals or to clothing.

Photo: Hugh Spencer

MAPLE FRUIT (above) It may sail on the wind across the fields to lodge in rich soil and grow into a tree.

Photo: Jopp-Monkemeyer

POPPY PODS (right) These pods are full of poppy seeds. When the wind blows and shakes them, they scatter the seeds to the ground through the tiny holes at the top.

Photo: Gregor-Monkemeyer

DANDELION SEEDS (above) Children often help to start dandelion seeds on their journey. Each fluffy parachute, which is easily carried by the wind, has a tiny seed attached to it.

Photo: L. W. Brownell

Photo: Monkemeyer

A RACCOON (above) Fur-bearing animals are of great importance to man, for the skins of many animals are used each year to make coats and other wearing apparel. The skins of cattle, horses, and other animals are used for making shoes and leather goods.

A PACK TRAIN (below) These sure-footed horses carry provisions and riders up the mountain trails. Horses are helpful to man in many ways. (See "Animals That Work for Man," in Volume Seven.)

Photo: Union Pacific Railroad

ELEPHANTS AT WORK (above) Man uses many kinds of animals to do his work. Elephants are often used in sawmills of Oriental countries to handle the logs. They can be taught to sort boards and to stack them in neat piles.

How Man Uses Animals and Plants

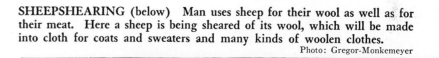

SHEEPSHEARING (below) Man uses sheep for their wool as well as for their meat. Here a sheep is being sheared of its wool, which will be made into cloth for coats and sweaters and many kinds of woolen clothes.

Photo: Gregor-Monkemeyer

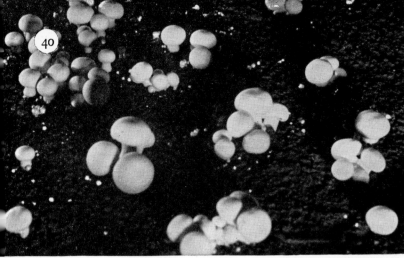

Photo: Butcher-Black Star

MUSHROOMS (above) Man uses many kinds of plants for food. Some mushrooms like the ones shown here are cultivated; these will be boxed and sold in stores.

A FIELD OF CABBAGES (below) Leaves, stems, roots, flowers, and seeds are all used for food. The leaves of cabbage, lettuce, and spinach, as well as many other leafy vegetables, are important plant foods for man.

Photo: L. W. Brownell

HAULING LOGS TO THE SAWMILL (below) These logs will be sawed into lumber to make houses, furniture, ships, and many other things.

Photo: Monkemeyer Press

Photo: Berger-Black Star

A FIELD OF CORN (above) This is only one of the crops farmers grow to supply food for man and for animals. The grains, or seeds, of many plants are ground into flour or meal for bread and similar foods.

TOMATOES (below, left) A fruit usually served as a vegetable.

BEANS (below, right) Seeds of plants are important as food. These pods contain the bean seeds, and enclose in sufficient food to feed the tiny growing plant. This stored food-material becomes food for man and animals.

Photo: D. V. Black Star   Photo: L. W. Brownell

Photo: L. W. Brownell

RASPBERRIES (above) A small fruit, which is important as a food. Fruits may be small like berries or nuts, or large, like grapefruit or apples.

HARVESTING PINEAPPLE (below) Tropical fruits and other foods are sent to the United States from distant countries; a great many ripe pineapples come from such plantations as this in Hawaii. They are also canned there and shipped to all parts of the world.

Photo: Monkemeyer Press

Photo: L. W. Brownell

THISTLE (above) Not only is this an un-comfortable plant to touch, but it is a bad weed, spoiling the farmer's crops of hay for his cattle. It is hard to destroy; and its seeds are winged so they can fly to distant places.

Photo: L. W. Brownell

POISON SUMAC (above) There are several varieties of sumac. The poisonous variety, sometimes called swamp sumac, is small and shrublike, with grayish bark, and bears white fruit. Handling it causes an itching rash. Sumacs with red berries are not poisonous.

Photo: L. W. Brownell

POISON IVY (above) This plant is easily recognized be-cause the leaflets grow in groups of three. The middle leaf has a stalk. The fruit is a white berry. The volatile oil given off by the plant often causes watery, itching blisters to form on the skin. Its leaves are bright red in fall.

Photo: Cornelia Clarke

WOOD NETTLE (above) This plant has many stinging hairs, and when they touch bare flesh they pro-duce an uncomfortable irritation. Consequently, man lets it alone.

POISONOUS MUSHROOMS Although some mushrooms are used for food, many kinds are extremely poisonous. These pictures show two poisonous ones: the poison amanita (below), or death cup, which is usually snowy white, and the fly amanita (lower left), which has an orange cap, spotted with white or pale-yellow scales. A dangerous mushroom is the russula (upper left) with its bright red top; it is found in damp woods all summer.

Plants Harmful to Man

HORSE NETTLE (below) This plant has rough, hairy leaves and white flowers, which later become shining purple berries. It is a troublesome weed and the berries contain a poisonous alkaloid.

Photo: L. W. Brownell

Photos: L. W. Brownell

MOUNT WILSON OBSERVATORY Years of careful experimentation have produced today's powerful telescopes. Scientists in many observatories have worked together to discover such facts as distances to the stars and planets, composition of the heavenly bodies, their movements and speeds, and their sizes and temperatures. Here is a picture of the large telescope located on Mount Wilson. It is a reflecting type of telescope with a mirror 100 inches in diameter. In this reflecting type of telescope no large lens is used. The rays of light from the heavenly body on which the telescope is focused strike the mirror and are brought together on a point. The light is then reflected and is seen through an eyepiece. Since large mirrors are much easier to make than large lenses the most powerful telescopes are "reflectors."

Photo: Museum of Science and Industry

Photo: Yerkes Observatory

Photo: Ewing Galloway

AN ANCIENT OBSERVER For centuries man has studied the heavens. Ancient man, thinking that the stars governed the lives of men, developed the pseudo-science of astrology. Gradually through more careful observation men noticed certain conditions such as the movements of the planets and the grouping of stars. From such knowledge as this has developed the oldest science in the world, astronomy. The lack of instruments delayed progress in astronomy, but when the first crude telescopes were developed the way was paved for the great discoveries of the future. The picture shows some of the first instruments used by observers of the heavenly bodies.

YERKES OBSERVATORY This refracting telescope uses lenses. When light strikes the lens it is bent so that it concentrates at one point. A large lens gathers a great deal of light and this makes it possible to see distant objects that could not be seen with the naked eye. This Yerkes Observatory telescope is located at Williams Bay, Wisconsin, and is one of the largest refracting telescopes in the world. The lens at the upper end is forty inches in diameter. As new and more powerful telescopes are made astronomers will find out more and more about the heavenly bodies. Already they can tell what stars are made of, how heavy they are, and many other interesting facts, in spite of the great distances between the nearest stars and the earth.

THE MOON

The moon is the earth's nearest neighbor in space and is only 240,000 miles away. It would take an airplane traveling 200 miles per hour only 50 days to reach it, whereas it would require over 50 years for the same plane to reach the sun. The moon travels around the earth once in every $27\frac{1}{3}$ days. Unlike the sun, it has no light of its own, but shines by reflected light from the sun. As the moon travels around the earth the sun lights only a part of it at a time. This makes the moon appear to change its shape from the crescent of a new moon to full moon (upper left) and then back to new moon again. "The new moon with the old moon in its arms" (upper center) merely means that the moon is visible by earth shine. Light is reflected from the sun to the earth and then to the moon and back to the earth again. No air nor water is on the moon and consequently no living things. The surface is rough, for it is covered with mountains and craters (lower left).

THE PLANETS

(See also diagram, page 45) The sun has a family of nine planets revolving around it. The five nearest the earth are visible with the naked eye; the others must be seen through a telescope. It would take an imaginary airplane, flying 200 miles per hour, 20 years to travel from the sun to Mercury; 39 years to Venus; 50 years to the earth; 82 years to Mars (below); 283 years to Jupiter; 513 years to Saturn (above); 1031 years to Uranus; 1600 years to Neptune; and to Pluto over 2000 years! The planets all get their light from the sun. Some are larger than others. As far as known there are no people on any of the other planets, although scientists think life might be able to exist on some of them. The song on page 110 of Volume Thirteen, "The Planets," teaches their names.

Photos: Yerkes Observatory

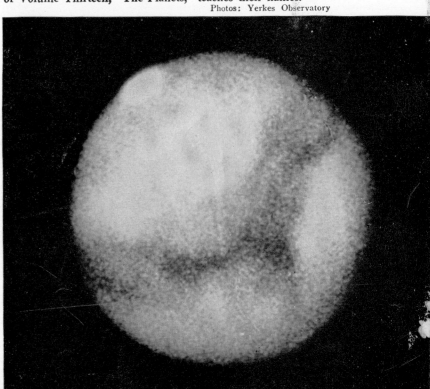

Photos: Yerkes Observatory

GREAT STAR CLOUD (above) Through the telescope countless numbers of stars like this can be seen. Close observation reveals that this cloud is actually composed of tiny specks that are really giant suns; they appear so small because they are so far away.

Observing the Heavens

SPIRAL NEBULA IN URSA MAJOR (above) This appears as a mass of glowing material. It is, in fact, however, really another galaxy like the Milky Way and is composed of stars. It is millions of miles in diameter and moves at a terrific speed.

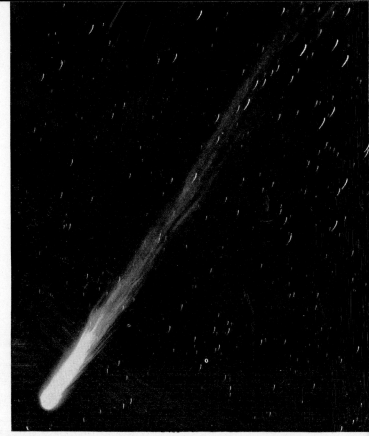

A COMET (above) Comets travel around the sun. Usually a comet consists of a head and a tail although the tail may be short. The head usually contains some solid material; the tail is composed of gaseous material. As the comet travels around the sun, the tail always points away from the sun. Several new comets are discovered each year.

URSA MAJOR (left) There are many groups of stars or constellations in the sky. This group, commonly called the Big Dipper, is one of the most easily recognized for it is always in our Northern sky. The two stars in the side of the dipper opposite the handle are called the pointers, and they point to the North Star.

A GASEOUS NEBULA (right) This view shows an expanse a thousand times as great as the distance from the earth to the sun. The cloudlike formations of this vast mass of gas consists of glowing oxygen and hydrogen. The atoms of the glowing gases are so far apart that they bump into one another about once in two years, whereas on the earth atoms of gas collide thousands of times every second.

The Solar System

Pluto

Neptune

Uranus

Venuso

Mercury

Earth

Mars

Saturn

Jupiter

Relative Distances of the Planets from the Sun

Sun Mercury Earth

Venus Mars

Jupiter

Saturn

Uranus

Neptune

Pluto

Relative Sizes of Planets Compared with the Sun

Jupiter

Saturn

Neptune

Uranus

Pluto Earth Venus Mars Mercury

Sun

K

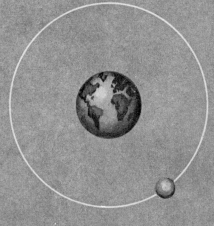

Relative Sizes of the
Earth and the Moon

Meteors

Frequently on clear nights one may see "shooting" or "falling stars." They are not really stars, for stars are of such great size that for one to fall would be a catastrophe beyond imagination. Note the meteor in the air (top left). Meteors are really small bodies which are not visible until they come into the earth's atmosphere, where they are heated by friction. They enter the earth's atmosphere at a tremendous speed—about thirty miles per second. A great number of meteors enter our atmosphere daily, but most of them are so small they are completely burned before they reach the ground. Sometimes, however, these bodies come

through the atmosphere and strike the earth. They are then known as meteorites. The diagram (left) shows how a meteorite came through the roof of a garage, the dotted line indicates its path; this meteorite (below) weighs about four pounds and is four and one-half inches at its widest part. Meteor Crater (lower left) is located in Arizona. The crater, nearly a mile in diameter and nearly six hundred feet deep, was made by a huge falling meteorite. Thousands of pieces of meteoric iron have been found around the crater. Look back at the picture of the moon, on page 43 and observe the craters there. Some astronomers believe that the craters on the moon were made by meteorites falling on it; others, however, believe that these are craters of extinct volcanoes. (See the opposite page.)

Photos: Field Museum of Natural History

Photo: Yerkes Observatory

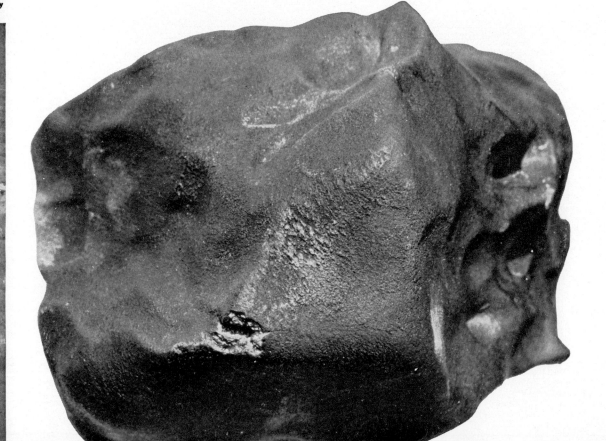

Photo: Damerel-F.P.G.

Photo: Ewing Galloway

A VOLCANO OF JAPAN (above) At one time in the history of the earth great changes were made by volcanoes. The explosions threw out volcanic ash and lava and built up huge cones, like this one—Fujiyama, the most perfect cone in the world.

The Face of The Earth Is Constantly Being Changed

WINTER DAMAGE (above) Snow and ice may change the form of trees during the winter. The weight of wet snow or ice on the limbs of trees is often more than the tree can support.

OLD FAITHFUL GEYSER (below) This geyser in Yellowstone National Park spouts a column of water 120 feet into the air at regular intervals of about sixty-seven minutes. Geysers change the earth's surface by leaving mineral deposits after the moisture has evaporated. Photo: Union Pacific Railroad

A GLACIER IN ALASKA (below) Glaciers change the face of the earth, slowly moving along, scraping and scouring the surface; and when they finally melt they deposit soil and rock in ridges called moraines. In North America many hills and valleys were formed by glaciers.

Photo: U. S. Geological Survey

Photo: Union Pacific Railroad

A NATURAL BRIDGE (above) This bridge has been carved from solid rock through long ages of erosion by wind and water. Wherever rock is exposed to the weather, its shape changes through these forces: wind blows sand against its face; water washes over it; and water freezes in the cracks and breaks the rock apart.

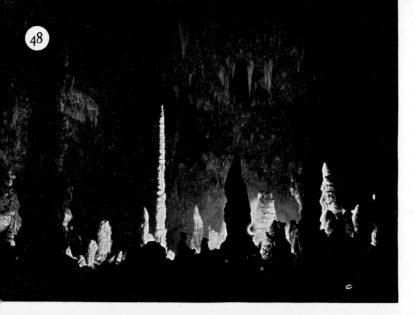

CARLSBAD CAVERNS, New Mexico, (top); CAMPBELL CAVERNS, near Sun Valley, Idaho, (bottom) These great rooms and underground halls were made as ground water dissolved the soil and rocks and carried them away. Through centuries the caves grew larger and longer until they became many miles long and hundreds of feet high. Dripping water containing lime and other minerals formed the iciclelike stalactites and built up stalagmites from the floor. Men have strung the electric lights to illuminate the walls so that visitors can now enjoy these underground wonders.

RIBBON FALLS IN GRAND CANYON (below) This stream of water is fed by springs. Note how the water has worn away the rock to make the huge opening and how the water falling on the rocks in the foreground has smoothed and worn them away.

Photos: Atchison, Topeka, and Santa Fe Railway, and Union Pacific Railroad

THE MIGHTIEST CHASM IN THE WORLD (above) This great gorge has been cut by the Colorado River, which may be seen in the center of the picture. The Grand Canyon is a mile deep and many miles long. A dipper of water from the river would contain hundreds of tiny grains worn from the canyon rocks. For centuries this wearing away has continued until the canyon appears as it does today.

THE OCEAN (above) Ocean waves beating upon the shore wear away the rocks. Sand bars are formed and washed away. Rocks are moved about. Cliffs crumble and portions of them slide into the sea.

EROSION (below) Scenes like this are common in the United States. Water running off the land has carried tons of top soil with it, leaving gullies. After this has gone on for a time the land becomes useless. Government agencies are now working to save the land by preventing this destructive erosion.

Photos: Ewing Galloway

Photo: Union Pacific Railroad

FALLS OF THE YELLOWSTONE RIVER (above) Rivers and waterfalls like this are continually changing the surface of the earth, wearing away the rocks over which they flow. After many years the river bed deepens and forms a canyon. It takes long periods of years to wear away mountains and to form deep valleys.

Photo: H. Armstrong Roberts

SAND DUNES (above) In many parts of the United States sand dunes like these have been built by the wind, whose force keeps shifting the dunes. Along Lake Michigan the winds have built dunes more than two hundred feet above the level of the lake.

The Face of The Earth Constantly Changed By Wind

EFFECTS OF WIND ON TREES Continuous blowing of the wind in one direction causes changes in the growth of plants, as shown by these palm trees (below, left) at St. Croix, Virgin Islands. The tree stump (below, center) has been carved by years of wind blowing sand against the trunk. Once it was almost covered by a sand dune. In Glacier National Park this tree (below, right) was deformed by the continuous force of the wind.

Photo: Keystone View

Photo: Union Pacific Railroad

WALL OF WINDOWS (above) In Bryce Canyon National Park the wind has blown sand against a wall of red, brown, and ochre rock, until it has been slowly worn into this lacelike form. Some rocks are less resistant to the effects of erosion than others and as a result holes were worn through the rocks and fantastic shapes created. Frost and heat have also helped the wind in its work.

Photo: Korth-Black Star

Photo: Ewing Galloway

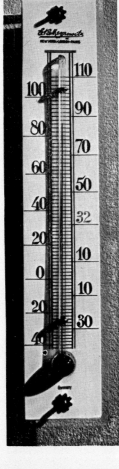

Weather

Weather is the condition from day to day of the blanket of air which surrounds the earth. Since the condition of this air changes hourly the weather condition also changes. Air may change in temperature and humidity, and as wind, which is merely air in motion, may change its direction. The pressure of the air changes, too. It is much to the advantage of man to be able to forecast these changes. Aviators and ship pilots need weather forecasts to anticipate storms and so plan safe journeys. Farmers and fruit growers depend on weather reports to prepare for frosts and heavy rains and save their crops from damage. Stockmen heed storm warnings by hurrying herds of animals to safety. Shippers need weather reports to prepare foods and other goods against freezing or spoiling. The United States Weather Bureau makes daily forecasts, broadcast over the nation, and publishes a daily weather map.

WIND SOCK (upper, left) and WIND TEE (center, left) One or the other of these is found on the air field to indicate direction of the wind and so guide pilots in take-offs and landings. The lights are for guidance at night. The tee is hollow and light and swings easily on its pivot.

THERMOMETER (above, center) This instrument commonly contains alcohol or mercury. Since liquids expand when heated and contract when cooled, they can be used to indicate temperatures. When the temperature increases, the liquid expands, rises into the tiny bore of the tube, and indicates the temperature. Temperatures of the air are usually given on a Fahrenheit scale. On the Fahrenheit thermometer freezing temperature is 32°, boiling is 212°; on the centigrade thermometer, 0° is freezing, 100° is boiling.

BAROMETER (below, left) This instrument, used extensively for weather forecasting, registers and indicates changes in air pressure. This is an aneroid barometer. Barometers are also filled with mercury, and the rising and falling of the column indicates changes in air pressure. The figures on this dial are given in "inches of mercury." The barometer indicates a pressure of 29.8, which means that the air pressure is sufficient to support a column of mercury 29.8 inches high. A falling barometer usually indicates a storm; a rising barometer means fair weather. Note the centigrade and Fahrenheit thermometers on the dial of the barometer.

WEATHER INSTRUMENTS (above) These are on the top of the building at the weather station to record temperature, amount of moisture in the air, air pressure, amount of sunshine, and other data necessary to use in forecasting weather conditions.

WEATHER VANE (below) This tells the direction from which the wind is blowing, helping to forecast the weather conditions. The direction changes frequently. This change may influence the temperature and thus effect a change in the amount of moisture, causing more evaporation or perhaps condensation. Sufficient cooling of humid air may cause rain or snow.

Photos: Ewing Galloway (except center, left) American Airlines

Photo: Ewing Galloway

AN AIRPLANE IN THE CLOUDS (above) A knowledge of clouds and cloud formations is important in forecasting weather. Clouds vary in altitudes, composition, and form. (See "Wonders of the Sky," in Volume Seven.)

There Are Many Kinds and Effects of Weather

CUMULUS CLOUDS (below) The type commonly seen in summer, often appearing prior to a local storm. Usually they are flattened at the bottom, and hang in the air nearly a mile above the earth.

Photo: Hugh Spencer

Photo: Hugh Spencer

ICICLES (above) When the water freezes it takes many forms. These icicles are formed when snow on the roof melts and the water drips from the eaves and refreezes. When rain drops are cooled below freezing as they fall they form sleet.

A GLACIER (below) Glaciers are formed as snow piles in the valleys of mountains to great depths. The pressure changes the lower layers to ice, and the ice begins to move outward and downward. Here is the end of a glacier; huge pieces of it will fall into the water and form icebergs.

Photo: Ewing Galloway

Photo: Harold M. Lambert

LIGHTNING AT NIGHT (above) The droplets of water in clouds become charged with electricity and when the charges leap, lightning flashes and thunder resounds.

SNOW (below) Snow blankets vegetation, keeps it from being winter-killed.

Photo: Lynwood M. Chace

Photo: Ewing Galloway

SNOW CRYSTALS (above) Snow forms in crystals of unusual designs. Here are a few of the beautiful patterns. Snow forms when moist air rises into the air and condenses at or below the freezing point.

FROST PATTERNS (below) Frost forms when the temperature at night falls below freezing and water vapor from the air condenses on chilled surfaces. Frost often appears on windows in beautiful designs like those shown here.

Photos: Lynwood M. Chace

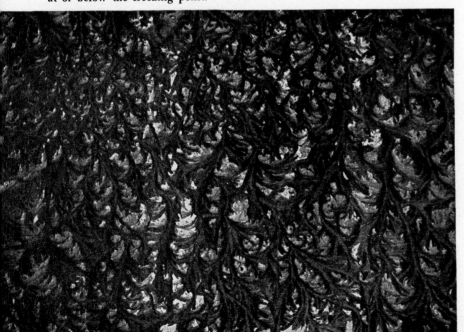

Photo: Lynwood M. Chace

DEW (above) When the temperature falls after sunset, dew may form on the grass and other surfaces, because the cool air cannot hold as much water vapor as the warm air of the day. Consequently some of the water vapor must be released, or condensed. Here dew has formed in huge drops on the twigs and other parts of a plant.

Photo: Ewing Galloway

RAIN CLOUD (above) Above the mountaintops and resting on them, the rain clouds gather. In this high region of the air the vapor cools, condenses, and falls as rain. Whence came the moisture of which these clouds are made? Mainly from the surface of the ocean waters, even though far away. Heat from the sun helped to evaporate the water and formed clouds, the wind drove them, and thus they reached this spot.

COLLECTION POOLS (above) During a heavy rainfall the water collects in little hollows or in deeper ones on the mountain's rugged surface, between the rocks, and at the bases of spongy moss beds. Wherever this collected water can find an unblocked passage downward, that is the way it goes. Such rain-water run-offs, or rills, are the beginnings of rivers-to-be.

MOUNTAIN TORRENT (above) Farther down from the summit a swift rivulet has formed.

The River—from Rain Cloud to Sea

THE WIDENING STREAM Flowing through grassy fields the stream, still swift but not dashing, merges with a creek (below, left). The rocks in the path of a mountain torrent are loosened, broken, and hurled onward by gravity's force and the momentum of the flow. Stones drop on the way as the load is carried along (lower, center). If this creek were dry, its rock-strewn bed would appear. In an old creek one may find interesting stones. Wider and shallower, farther along its course, the creek shows its gravelly bottom (lower, right). In the time of high water, in spring, without doubt many of the stones will move on. The power of the rushing streams has been sufficient to move great stones and gradually to wear away their irregular shapes until they are round and smooth. The stream looks quiet enough now; but a dramatic moment approaches.

THE FALLS (below) The creek takes a plunge, a sheer drop of many feet; it is the beautiful phenomenon called a waterfall.

Photos (6): H. Armstrong Roberts

Photo: Lynwood M. Chace

SPEED AND POWER (above) The river at the rapids, almost as if armed with hammer, crowbar, shovel, chisel, and file, reshapes and dislodges rocks, and levels the hollows they leave in the mud; it uproots dead trees from the shores and hurls them onward.

AN OLD STREAM (left) Sluggishly, meandering around obstructions instead of dashing across them or breaking them down. Slow streams widen the valleys, silt fills their channels, and low-lying plains are formed. Only in times of flood does the river cover its flats.

Photo: Harold M. Lambert

THE CREEK (above) Free of boulders and other obstacles the creek flows onward, soon to join a river. This farmland scene shows the water going over a small dam.

A GUARD (below) Standing on the bridge at night the harbor guard scans the river's murky waters.

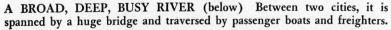

A BROAD, DEEP, BUSY RIVER (below) Between two cities, it is spanned by a huge bridge and traversed by passenger boats and freighters.

THE RIVER (above) The creek at last has flowed into the river. The gateway, or notch, in these mountains was cut by this river during eons of time.

MOUTH (below) Some rivers, such as this one, meet a depression of the land at their mouth, and a bay is formed. Through the waters of the bay the river will reach the sea. And so the cycle goes on. Moisture from the ocean falls as rain on the land. Rain water gathers into larger and larger streams, gravity-moved and ocean-bound.

Photos (5): H. Armstrong Roberts

Photo: Fred T. Loomis

A GLIDER (above) By steering a glider into rising air currents, a skillful pilot can keep it in the air for hours. Unlike an airplane, the glider has no engine or propeller.

Force of Air

A WINDMILL (below) The force of wind is turning the windmill and pumping water from the ground. In some countries the force of the wind is used in this manner to grind grain.

Photo: Ewing Galloway

Photo: Ewing Galloway

A PARACHUTE JUMP (above) A parachute is opened by the air and buoyed up as the aviator falls, so that his descent is not too rapid.

TOY BALLOONS (below) Air-filled balloons are often used to tell the direction of the wind.

Photo: Free-Lance Photographers Guild

Photo: Made on Agfa Film

FLYING SPINNAKERS (above) The force of wind has played a most important role in man's water transportation. Riding ahead of the wind, he has been able to carry heavy loads across the waters of lakes, rivers, and oceans. The sails can be set so that the boat can travel against the wind as well as with the wind. Nowadays sailboats are most frequently used for pleasure, since steam as a force has taken the place of wind. (See page 58.)

Photo: Ewing Galloway

Photo: General Electric

DIRIGIBLE (above) The dirigible is run by motors, which drive the propellers. It is steered by the rudder. It is long and pointed so that it can be driven into the wind. The gas inside the dirigible is lighter than air.

A WINCHARGER (below) Moving water is not the only force that can be used to generate electricity. The blades (center) are turned by the wind and run a generator that makes electricity. Farmers who are not near an electric line but have a Wincharger can then use the many devices run by electricity so generated.

Photos: Wincharger Corp.; Post-Dispatch from Black Star; Zenith Radio

VACUUM CLEANER (above) The vacuum cleaner is run by air pressure; the force of the wind created by air pressure carries dirt into the cleaner as it is moved back and forth over the rug.

Photo: Eisenmeier-F.P.G.

KITEFLYING (above) Any windy day is good kiteflying weather because the force of the wind blowing under the kite keeps it aloft. By running the boy starts it flying upward. A tail helps to balance it, so that it will stay steadily aloft.

THE RAPIDS (above) The force of moving water is carrying these boats rapidly downstream. Men not only use wind force, but also water force to aid them in their travels. It takes skill to handle a boat in swift waters.

Force of Water

TURBINE (below) This machine, operated by steam, a form of water, generates electricity.

Photo: Ewing Galloway

Photo: Ewing Galloway

STEAM The force of water is of great importance to man. Running water turns water wheels and runs power turbines that generate electricity. Water changed to steam has great force, and this force is used to run a locomotive (right). An engineer is putting coal into the fuel box (above) where the heat from the burning coal will change the water into steam. The steam becomes a mighty power—a giant in a box—causing the piston of the engine to move back and forth (right). This movement is transferred to the wheels to make them turn and pull the train.

Photo: Harold M. Lambert

A MILL WHEEL (above) Running water turns the wheel, and its shaft turns other wheels; this force may be used to grind grain, saw wood, or do other kinds of work.

Photo Popular Mechanics

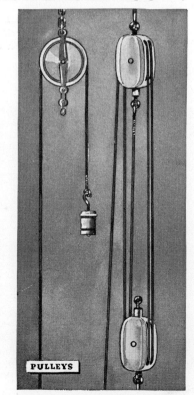

WHEEL

Every day we use many different kinds of machines for many different purposes: to lift things, to pry them loose and to split them apart, to mix them, and to carry them to different places. Some machines we use are very simple; others are very complicated.

On this page are pictured some of the simple machines that are commonly used. The *wheel and axle* is one of the oldest simple machines man invented to help him in his work. Wheels are used to pull heavy loads from place to place. Egg beaters, clothes wringers, bicycles, gear wheels, and automobile steering wheels are some of the more complex ways in which wheels are commonly used. (For illustrations of ways in which wheels are used, see page 60.)

Pulleys are also simple machines and are used for many purposes. One kind of pulley, known as the fixed pulley, is used to raise a flag to the top of a pole. Another type is the movable pulley, shown in various machines on the following pages.

Pulleys are often arranged as shown here—an arrangement called a block and a tackle. They make work easier, as shown in the picture of the motorboat on page 61. Other kinds of pulleys, such as the cable car, are shown on page 61.

Another type of simple

PULLEYS

SIMPLE MACHINES

"Man is a tool-making animal."
—BENJAMIN FRANKLIN

machine is the *lever.* There are different kinds of levers. When you use a pry to move a stone out of the ground you are using a lever. Shears, pliers, a wheelbarrow, a pump handle, the oars of a boat, a hammer, a nutcracker, a seesaw, and a crowbar are some of the different examples of levers in daily use. (See page 63 for illustrations of levers.)

Another kind of simple machine is the *inclined plane.* It is often used in loading heavy boxes and barrels into cars. Circus animals and wagons are put into railway cars by the use

LEVERS

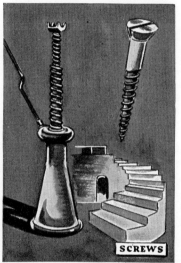

LEVERS

of an inclined plane. A staircase, a winding mountainous road, a ramp in a garage, a slanting floor in a theater are all examples of inclined planes. (Some of these examples are illustrated on page 64.)

The *screw* is another simple machine. Screws may also be called twisted inclined planes. A circular stairway illustrates the similarity. Screws are used to hold materials together as in furniture or in watches, to

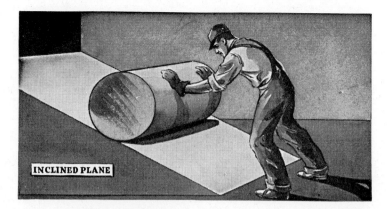

INCLINED PLANE

raise cars (jack), in faucets to turn on water, in meat grinders, and in a bit to bore holes. (For illustrations see page 62.)

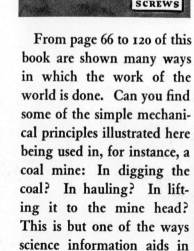

SCREWS

The *wedge* is also a simple machine. It is used to split things apart. A snowplow, an axe, and a chisel are examples of a wedge which is really two inclined planes attached together. (See page 64 for illustrations of these examples.) The following pages will show some of the uses of simple machines and also of more complex machines.

From page 66 to 120 of this book are shown many ways in which the work of the world is done. Can you find some of the simple mechanical principles illustrated here being used in, for instance, a coal mine: In digging the coal? In hauling? In lifting it to the mine head? This is but one of the ways science information aids in the study of industry.

WEDGE

THE SOLID WHEEL (above) Wheels have been used for thousands of years. One of the earliest types must have been much like this wheel still used on ox carts in Oriental countries today. Compare it with the modern wheels on this page.

The Wheel—An Important Invention of Man

THE WHEELBARROW (below) This is really a kind of lever combined with a wheel; and here it is being wheeled up and down an inclined plane.

WHEEL WITH AXLE (above) Man has made many changes in wheels since the first solid wheels were made. The axle here can be greased to run smoothly.

GEAR WHEELS (below) Gear wheels are used in egg beaters, clothes wringers, bicycle sprockets; automobiles and more complicated machines are made up of many gear wheels. What other machines have gear wheels?

LANDING GEAR OF FAST TRANSPORT PLANE (above) The twin wheels with their great rubber tires absorb much of the shock of landing the heavy plane.

ENGINE WHEEL (below) The force of steam drives this wheel along the rails. It must be all steel to stand the terrific weight and pull of the train.

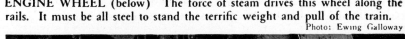

Photo: Goro-Monkemeyer

LOWERING A HEAVY BOAT (above) The block and tackle as pictured here can be used to lift heavy loads with small force. The greater the number of strands of rope that support the movable pulley the greater the mechanical advantage. Many elevators in mines, on the sides of new buildings, in factories, and wherever great loads must be lifted have pulley systems of similar construction.

Photo: Mayer-Black Star

A CABLE CAR (above) Pulleys run along this cable and carry the car and its load across the mountains. One fixed and one moving wheel makes one of the simplest types of pulley combinations.

DREDGE (below) Pulleys find many and varied uses in this machine, which digs great loads of dirt from the bottom of the river.

Photo: Ewing Galloway

Photo: Ewing Galloway

GIANT SHOVEL (above) This compound machine uses levers, pulleys, wheels, and other kinds of simple machines to lift loads.

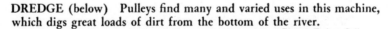

The Pulley—Used To Pull And Lift Big Loads

BELTS AND PULLEYS (below) These are often used to transmit the force of one machine to another part of the machine or to some other machine. A twisted belt will reverse the direction in which the second pulley runs.

Photo: Lambert-Black Star

Photo: Keystone View

JACKSCREW (above) Here a screw is used to lift a heavy automobile. Jackscrews are often used to lift whole buildings when they must be moved. This screw is really a kind of inclined plane, as explained on page 59.

The Screw—Made To Lift Great Weights

Photo: Freida Zylstra

DRIVING A SCREW (above) This tool is being driven into the wood. The boy's hands give the power, or force, and the bit, which is a type of screw, cuts easily into the wood.

SCREWS IN A WATCH (below) Although screws are used to lift heavy weights, minute screws, some so tiny that a teacup would contain millions of them, hold the parts of a watch together. It is because they will not pull out or jar loose that screws are so used.

Photo: Saturday Evening Post

SCREW PART ON A DAM (below) This machinery is used to open and close the gates of a dam. The arrow points to the screw.

Photo: Larsen-Black Star

Photo: Ewing Galloway

CONSTRUCTING FURNITURE (above) A workman using a machine-driven bit to make a round hole in the wood. As the bit, the screw part, turns it takes out the wood. Screws are also used to make holes in iron, but greater force must be put behind them.

Photo: U. S. Department of Agriculture

STACKING HAY (above)   A lever is here used to place hay on the stack.   The force is supplied by the use of pulleys.   Horses give the needed pull to start the pulleys working.

OARS IN A BOAT (below)   These oars are levers.   Although the boat is the weight being moved, it is done by pushing against the water.   The force is transmitted through the oars and the boat is thus moved through the water.

Photo: H. Armstrong Roberts

Photo: Lynwood M. Chace

A DRAW WELL (above)   Here a simple lever is used to draw water from an open well.   With such a long handle at one end, very little force lifts the heavy bucket at the short end.

THE SHOVEL (below)   This is also a lever. Force at the top of the handle lifts soil from the ground at the edge of the shovel.   The fulcrum is the point on which the shovel is braced.

Photo: U. S. Department of Agriculture

Photo: Balcolm-Carmody—Black Star

A TEETER-TOTTER (above)   This is a simple lever.   If children are of unequal weights, they soon learn to balance each other by moving closer to or farther from the fulcrum, or pivoting point.

The Lever—Controls Many Useful Appliances

THE PUMP HANDLE (below)   This handle is a lever similar to the one at a draw well.   Air pressure in a modern lift pump forces the water through the spout instead of man's having to lift a heavy bucket with the lever.

Photo: Ewing Galloway

REPAIRING THE CLOCK (above) Here are many different kinds of tools: wedges, levers, wheels and axles, screws, and inclined planes. Each serves its special purpose, as every child who has used them knows.

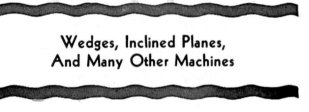

Wedges, Inclined Planes, And Many Other Machines

A MODERN KITCHEN (below) When you turn the faucet to get a drink, you make use of the simple machine known as a screw. The work-saving devices in a kitchen contain many other simple machines, such as wheels, pulleys, wedges, and levers. See how many simple machines you can find in your kitchen.

HAMMER AND CHISEL (above) This boy is using a chisel as a wedge to cut a hole in this block of wood. The hammer drives the wedge in, causing the wood to split.

SLEDDING (below) Gravity pulls the sled down this inclined plane. A mountain road and a flight of stairs are both inclined planes.

THE WEDGE (above) This tool has a great variety of uses. Here it is employed to split a slab from a log too large for the circular saw. An axe is also a wedge.

INCLINED PLANE (below) These heavy bales of cotton can be loaded much more easily by using planks as an inclined plane. Most gangplanks are inclined planes.

INTRODUCTION TO INDUSTRY SECTION

Children of today live in a machine age; they hear the roar of machines from the airplanes above, from the trains and automobiles on the surface, and, in great cities, from the subway beneath; they stand fascinated as they watch the wheels of industry revolve, crushing and grinding or bringing some raw material into a product useful in social life. They are challenged to invent, create, construct in an experience of their own. They admire their own crude but precious products.

Frank and Alice live on a farm. They take an active part in the farm community. In the early spring, machines come out to plow, to sow grain, to cultivate plants, to harvest crops. Where do all the products of the farm go? Frank jumps on the motor truck loaded with tomatoes. He goes to a near-by cannery. There he finds more machines, and busy men and women at work. He returns with his story of the canning of tomatoes. His father shows him these pictures of Industry to supplement his experiences.

Alice helps her mother in the kitchen. She sees an automatic machine mixing dough that will soon become bread. Mother removes the dough from the large earthen bowl in which it was mixed and pushes the bowl too close to the edge of the table. Crash goes the bowl! Alice picks up the pieces. She looks at the powder that came from a crushed piece of the bowl. "How do you make bowls, Mother?" "Ask your teacher," answers her busy mother.

The next day, "Where do dishes come from?" she asks her teacher. "We shall look for clay in the ditch along the stream and then I will help you to understand." When the teacher and children had brought some of the "tough, sticky earth" to the classroom, each child made a bowl. But they were not beautiful and shiny like the broken one. Alice's teacher then showed the children in the pictures of Industry the many processes necessary to make a big, shiny, colorful mixing bowl.

A trip to the city is planned. Off they go! Frank and Alice and their father are taking baskets of apples to market. The road gets bumpy as they approach the state highway. A man stands with the red flag. The car stops. An explosion is heard in the distance. "What is it?" cries Alice. "Only blasting of rock," says father. "Don't you see a road is being made?" On goes the car. Father keeps to one side of the road. Noise, noise! A machine is chugging, rocks are being crushed. The cement mixer is near by. A new road is being made. "How do you make cement, Father?" "We'll see when we return. We'll watch the men a little longer; and then we shall look at the pictures of Industry."

Episodes in the lives of children should be supplemented by pictures and stories. Children are interested in the world in which they live. Parents and teachers can make these events thrilling adventures when they become acquainted with these pictures of Industry.

The pictures were selected by a group of three educators: Edith Osswald, teacher in the Woodward School, Brooklyn, New York; Helena Wilson, Principal of the Oran M. Roberts School in Houston, Texas; and Mary M. Reed, Emeritus Assistant Professor of Education at Teachers College, Columbia University. Lillian Sessoms, a former teacher of young children, now active in literary research, assisted in writing the captions. From many hundreds of pictures the group selected pictures for their interest to young children: pictures which tell the best story, pictures which fit best into a curriculum, and pictures not found in other books, nor easily obtainable by teachers in current literature. Every effort was made by the whole group working on this project to express through the captions accurate information in a literary form suitable for use with children of the primary grades.

MARY M. REED, Emeritus Assistant Professor of Education
Teachers College, Columbia University

Photo: U. S. Department of Agriculture

Photo: J. I. Case Company

Agriculture

The greatest industry in America is agriculture. From the farms come the products of field, garden, and orchard for food; livestock for meat; cotton, wool, and linen for clothing; hides for leather. Here are shown a few of the many tasks in the preparation of products for market.

PLOWING AND PULVERIZING In early spring furrows are cut through the earth where crops grew the year before. The ground must be broken up and thoroughly cultivated before any new seed is sown. Small fields are usually plowed with horses or mules (above, left). Large fields are often plowed with a tractor (below, left). After a field has been plowed, generally a disk harrow (above, right)

is used to break up the ground before seeding. Its sharp, revolving disks are drawn back and forth across the field, pulverizing the ground. The disk harrow is angled and straightened by tractor power. **PLANTING** (below, right) The farmer and his son are filling the hopper of a cotton planter with seed. The planter drops 5 or 6 seeds in a single line at regular intervals 10 to 12 inches apart.

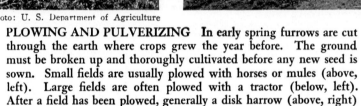

Photo: J. I. Case Company

Photo: U. S. Department of Agriculture

Photos: J. I. Case Company (two above)

CULTIVATING (above, left) After seed is planted, the soil must be tilled and the weeds kept down. In large fields this is done by cultivators—a series of small plowshares drawn by a tractor. This cornfield is being cultivated in Indiana in mid-July.

HAYMAKING When the hay has grown tall enough the farmer mows it, the tractor-drawn hay baler (above, right) gathers the hay, slices it, and packs it into easily handled bales. The old way was to rake the hay and stack it on horse-drawn carts (below, right).

THE CROP (below, left) The leader of a Four-H Club explains to the boys how good ears of corn will appear when they are full-grown and the crop is ready for harvesting when autumn comes.

FRUIT PICKING (below, center) Not all crops grow in the fields; this girl is helping to gather the pear crop in the orchard. She lays each pear carefully in the bucket so the fruit will not bruise and spoil.

Photos: **U. S.** Department of Agriculture (three below)

Food Preservation

TOMATOES AT THE CANNERY (above) From near-by farms come hundreds of baskets of ripe tomatoes to the cannery. The tomatoes are carefully graded according to quality and size before being canned.

GRAPEFRUIT CANNERY (below) Women peel the grapefruit by hand and put them into wire baskets, which travel on a conveyor to the workers at the extreme right, who core the fruit, separate and peel the segments, and fill the cans. The conveyor moves the filled cans through the closing machine (upper right). A workman is inserting a new supply of lids. Sealed cans are submerged and sterilized in these huge kettles (lower right) at about 180° Fahrenheit.

Photos: American Can Company

QUICK-FROZEN FOODS Many foods are frozen, including vegetables, fruits, meat, fish, and poultry. Here are the steps in the quick-freezing of peas. Pea vines, cut close to the ground by mowing machines are automatically loaded onto a truck (above, left) and rushed to the packing plant. Here machines remove the peas from their vines and pods. When the boxes (above, center) are filled, the peas are ready for the machines in which they are washed a number of times (above, right). Every effort is made to have the peas perfect. Girls pick out all imperfect peas and any remaining waste (below, left corner). The peas are put into the wax-board boxes and weighed within a fraction of an ounce (below, left center). Now they are ready for the quick-freezing machines (below, right center), deep cabinets divided by aluminum shelves. When the cabinet is full, the shelves move upward, pressing the boxes between them and squeezing out most of the air from each package. Then the heavy doors are closed. An extremely cold liquid substance circulates inside the shelves, quickly freezing the peas at sub-zero temperatures. After about an hour and a half, they are completely frozen and are ready to be placed in the cold-storage room (below, right corner). All freshness, fragrance, and flavors are sealed in until the foods are served.

Photos: Frosted Food Sales Corporation

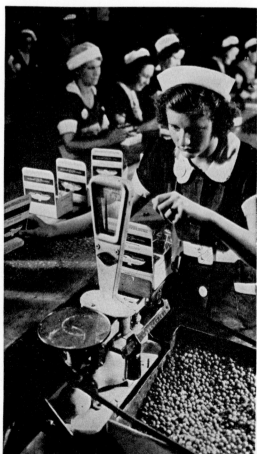

Plastics

Strong, colorful plastics are used to make hundreds of different kinds of articles, from toys to telephones. There are many kinds of plastics especially suited to various uses. Plastics are made from cotton and wood fibers, and from acids and other chemicals. Some are made from coal, petroleum, air, and water. In the typical plastics-making process, the raw materials are first combined to form a substance called a synthetic resin.

HOT RESIN (left) flows from the kettle after the raw materials have been thoroughly mixed and cooked.

THE COOLED RESIN (right) is broken into small pieces like lumps of coal. Then it is ground to a fine powder and loaded into drums. This powder is called a molding compound.

Photos: Durez Plastics; Pro-phy-lac-tic; Monsanto

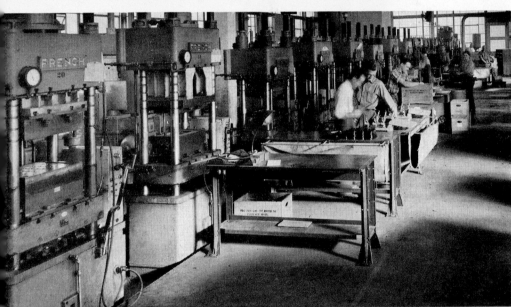

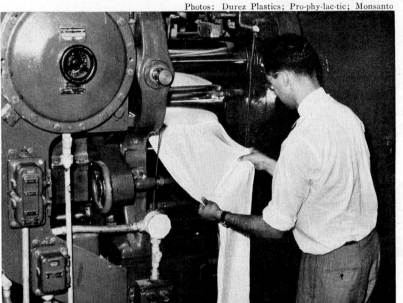

COMPRESSION MOLDING (second left) These machines work like waffle irons. The powered resin, or molding compound, is poured into a mold which is the shape of the article to be made. Then heat and pressure are applied until the plastic has hardened. The machines we see here are making plastic toothbrush handles.

CALENDERING (left) In this process, a thin coating of heat-softened plastic is applied to cloth. The machine then presses and smoothes the cloth between a series of rollers, until the plastic is thoroughly worked into the fibers. The plastic called synthetic rubber is often used in calendering. Some raincoats are made of calendered cloth.

LAMINATING (second left) is like making a sandwich, with the plastic as the filling. Here we see a huge press which makes these plastic sandwiches. First several thin sheets of wood, called veneer, are placed together with a sticky kind of plastic between them. Then the sheets are placed in the big press and squeezed together at high temperature. After the plastic has hardened, it holds the sheets of wood together. They have now become plywood, a tough building material.

EXTRUDING (left) is much like squeezing toothpaste out of a tube. Heat-softened plastic is forced through an opening to form it into the desired shape. Tubes, rods, and many other plastics products are manufactured in this way.

Leather

Leather is made from the hides of animals. Usually the hides of cattle, horses, sheep, pigs, and goats are used. But sometimes fine leathers are manufactured from the skins of various other animals, such as snakes, alligators, sharks, and ostriches.

TANNING is the first step in making leather, after the hair has been removed from the hides. The tanning liquid is made from the bark of oaks and certain other trees. It makes the hides tough and keeps them from decaying. After the hides are soaked in this liquid, they are put through wringers (upper left) to squeeze them dry.

SPLITTING LEATHER (upper right) The next step is to split the hides into even thicknesses. Some kinds of leather also are shaved, to give them a finer and smoother finish. Then the hides are hung over poles and carried through a heated tunnel to the massaging room.

MASSAGING THE HIDES (lower left) The leather is softened by massaging it with these machines, which the operators guide. Leather must be made soft so that it will not crack when it is used.

STRETCHING (lower right) After the hides have been massaged, they are stretched and tacked on boards so that they will be smooth and flat when they reach the workers who finish the leather.

Photos: Armour Leather Company

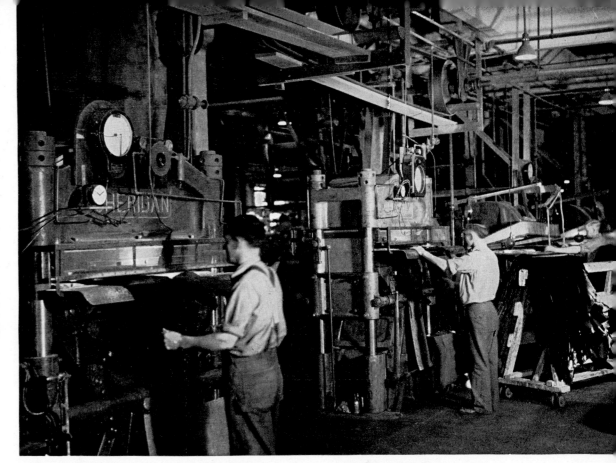

HAND FINISHING (above) Fancy leathers are finished by hand. The leatherworkers here are coloring hides.

MACHINE FINISHING (upper right) Leather can be given different finishes. This hydraulic press gives the leather a smooth finish and sometimes embosses designs on it.

MEASURING (below) Hides are of such irregular shapes that there must be a special machine for measuring them. As they are run through this machine the wheels that touch the leather revolve and automatically register the area on the dial.

SORTING (lower right) The finished leather is sorted according to weight, quality, color, and finish.

Photos: The Armour Leather Company

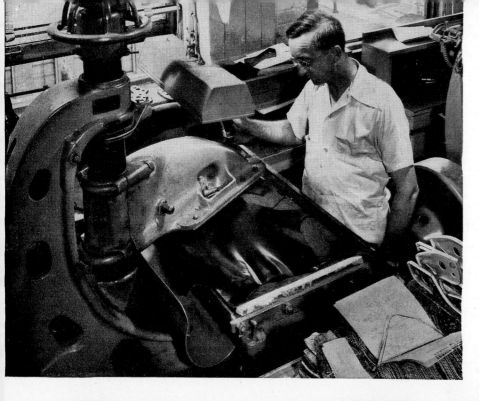

SHOEMAKING

Leather is most important in making shoes. It is elastic enough to be comfortable to the feet and porous enough to allow air to get through it. More than 200 operations are involved in making a single shoe. Only a few of them can be shown here. The chief operations include cutting, stitching, heel and sole shaping, assembling, bottoming, heel attaching, finishing, and final cleaning and dressing.

CUTTING THE LEATHER (left) The required pieces of leather are cut out by accurate machines.

PERFORATING (right) Designs for various parts and eyelets for the laces are punched by machine.

ASSEMBLING (below) In the lasting room various shoe parts are assembled and shaped on the last.

INSEAMING (below right) This operation takes place before the uppers and soles are attached.

Photos: Nunn-Bush Shoe Co.; The Cooley Co.

Wool

CLIPPING WOOL (below) Sheep are usually clipped once a year; in warm countries, twice. Estimates vary as to the number of sheep that can be clipped in a day, depending on the shearer and the sheep. The fleece of one sheep weighs from three to five pounds. Wool is used for clothing because it holds the heat of the body well. Sometimes wool is mixed with cotton to make the cloth stronger but the cloth will not be so warm. (For hand shearing see page 39.)

MAKING WOOLEN YARN (upper right) After the wool has been washed and carded so that the fibers are loosened, it is twisted and drawn into yarn of the desired size by a machine called a mule.

WEAVING WOOLEN CLOTH (lower right) These are the weaving machines where woolen yarn is woven into cloth. (See also page 77.)

Photo: H. Armstrong Roberts (below)

Photos: Ewing Galloway (above), Pacific Mills (below)

Cotton

PICKING COTTON BY HAND These people earn their living for many weeks of the year by picking cotton. They are paid according to the number of pounds they pick. Some become skilled cotton pickers and work very rapidly. Many Negroes are fast pickers; they are especially adapted for this work because they are able to endure the intense heat of the Southern sun.

As the pickers take the cotton from its stem, they drop it into the sacks that hang by straps from their necks (below). These bags are then dumped upon the larger burlap sacks spread flat on the ground. When the sacks are full, the cotton is weighed (upper, left) by the overseer or manager of the plantation before being loaded into wagons and carried to the gin (page 76).

PICKING COTTON BY MACHINE (lower left) Inventors worked for many years to make a successful cotton-picking machine. It usually takes a hand picker a full day to gather 150 to 250 pounds of cotton. The mechanical picker can gather several thousand pounds of the fluffy white bolls in a day. Special kinds of cotton have been developed which are easy to pick by machine. They grow to an even height, and all the bolls ripen at the same time.

Photos: Ewing Galloway (upper left and below)

Photo: International Harvester

WHITNEY'S COTTON GIN (below) Eli Whitney, an ingenious Yankee farmer boy, was persuaded by a Southern plantation owner to try his hand at inventing a machine for removing the seeds from cotton. At that time the seeds had to be picked by hand from the fluffy white cotton fibers, and even the fastest picker could not clean more than a few pounds a day. Whitney's machine combed the cotton with wires so that the fibers fell into one compartment, the seeds into another.

Cotton seeds are useful not only for planting but also as a source of oils used in cooking and, when pressed into blocks, as feed for cattle.

A MODERN GIN (upper right) Cotton is carried from the fields in trucks. At the gin it is lifted from the trucks by suction pipes. Today all cotton is ginned by machinery; hundreds of pounds are cleaned of their seeds in a day's time. Then it is ready to be packed into bales. Most of the modern gins are based on the same principle of the wire comb that Whitney invented.

COTTON BALES (lower right) After ginning, the cotton is packed under great pressure into bales containing about 500 pounds. Machines cover it with burlap and bind it with metal strips. The cotton is now ready to be shipped to all parts of the world, to be woven into cloth, or to be used for many other purposes.

Photo. Museum of Science and Industry (below, left)

Photos: Ewing Galloway (above); Goodyear Tire and Rubber Company (below)

SPINDLES (upper left) Spindles twist fibers into threads. The "large thread" of partly twisted cotton fibers passes into the top of the spindle, down the side, and is then given a twist as it is wound onto the spindles. Each twist makes it firmer and more like the thread used for sewing or the yarn used for weaving.

WARP (lower left) To make the warp of cotton cloth, the yarn must be wound onto beams, or huge rolls. The threads are evenly spaced as they are wound; at the same time they are covered with a protective coating to resist the action of the shuttle and to hold the threads in place.

LOOMS (below) In this great weaving room the warp is running from the beams through the looms while the shuttles fly back and forth, weaving the thread into cloth. Weavers call this thread "the filling." Formerly, cotton-cloth factories were usually located in Northern cities, far from the plantations where cotton grows; today factories are built in cities near the cotton fields.

Photo: Ewing Galloway (below)

Photos: Pepperell Manufacturing Company (above and below)

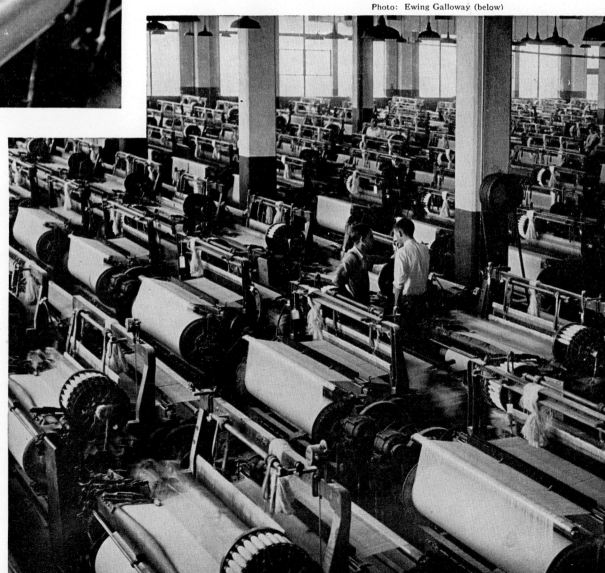

A RIPPLER (below) The man is drawing flax through the big spikes on the board to pull apart its fibers, thus separating them from the seeds. The iron comb is called a rippler. Next the flax is retted, or soaked, to loosen the fiber from the decaying woody part of the stalk. Machinery is gradually supplanting the hand-rippling process. A bushel of seeds yields about seventeen to twenty pounds of linseed oil. Linseed meal, the residue, is a valuable feed for cattle.

Photos: International Harvester; Ewing Galloway

Linen

HARVESTING FLAX (above) Flax is the plant from whose fiber linen is made and from whose seed linseed oil is pressed. It grows in a cool, damp climate and reaches two or three feet in height. A flat field in bloom with small, nodding, blue flowers looks like a reflection of the sky.

When raised for its seed it is harvested when quite ripe. Harvesting used to be done by hand; today one machine threshes out the flaxseed and ties the stalks for drying. When cultivated for its fiber, flax is harvested before complete ripening. The best fibers, found on the inner side of the stem bark next to a central woody core, are frequently pulled by hand and tied in bundles set upright in the fields until dry.

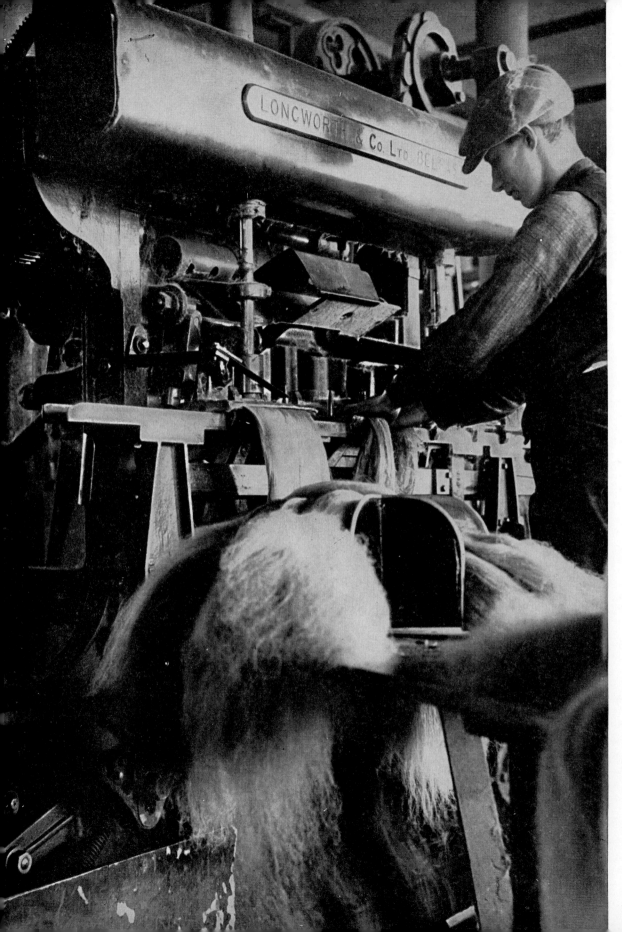

HACKLING (left) To release flax fiber from the stem, it is cut lengthwise by a scutching blade or a scutching machine. This breaks the hard stem into pieces, leaving the fiber intact. Before the flax can be spun, it is hackled. The hackling machine shown here straightens out and cleans the fibers by clawing through them with small pins set on a revolving belt. This claw pulls out the short fibers and leaves the long ones parallel. The short fibers, called tow, are used in the manufacture of coarse, cheap linen and rope.

LINEN WEAVING (below) Flax fibers removed from the roving machine, which draws them to a uniform thickness, are passed through warm water on their way to the spinning machine. The spinning machine pulls out the fibers still farther and twists them into thread. Before being woven into cloth the thread must be bleached. In weaving, either by hand or by machine, the linen threads must be kept wet to prevent their breaking. This factory is in Belfast, Ireland.

One of the properties of linen cloth is its strength. For this reason it is used extensively in the manufacture of airplane cloth, sailcloth, and canvas. On the other hand, linen can be spun so fine that handkerchiefs and other dainty and expensive goods are made of this cloth. Linen has been woven for thousands of years. The Egyptians used to wrap their mummies in long strips of linen cloth, and the priests in Babylon, Egypt, and Judea wore fine linen.

Photos: Ewing Galloway

Silk

SILKWORMS (right) Silkworms are not really worms but are caterpillars of the silk moth. They feed upon the leaves of the white mulberry tree which grows best in China and Japan. The female attaches her eggs to a leaf or similar surface. When hatched, the caterpillars are about a quarter-inch long; they feed for some eight weeks, changing their skins four times. When about three inches long, they spin cocoons of silky threads (below, left). A cocoon used for silk must be heated to kill the chrysalis within; if the moth should emerge as shown here, the threads would be broken and the cocoon useless for silk-making. Water dissolves the gummy substance holding the threads together; then the rough outer threads are brushed off. Now the fine inner filaments are reeled off, a most delicate task. Several thousand yards are in a cocoon; only 350 to 750 yards can be reeled into skeins. The filaments of several cocoons are wound off together. The skeins of yellowish filaments are called raw silk.

Photos: Russell H. Anderson (upper right and below); Ewing Galloway (lower right)

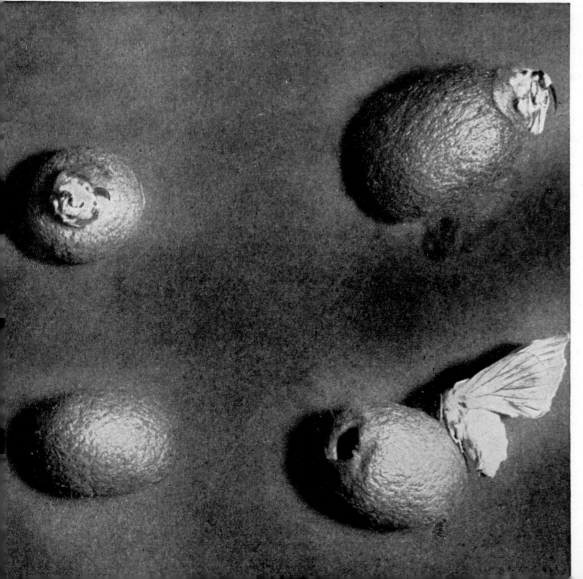

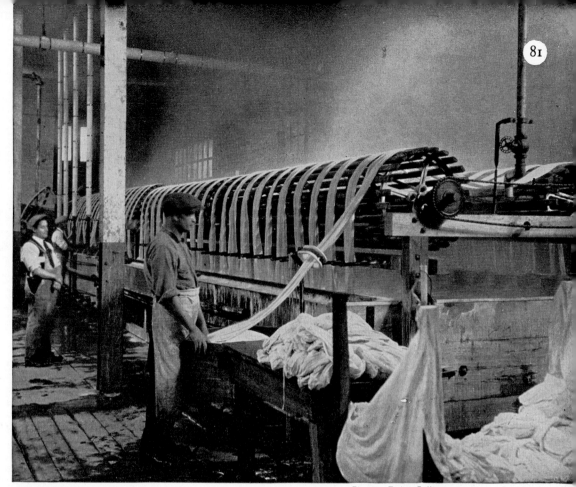

Photos: Ewing Galloway

WEAVING (page 80, lower right) The United States buys much raw silk and has many mills where the silk is made into spool thread, cloth, hosiery and other knitted goods. Paterson, New Jersey, is the center of the silk industry. This man is weaving silk cloth at a harness loom.

A STOCKING MILL (upper left) This picture shows knitting machines making full-fashioned stockings. They must be sewed up before they look like stockings. One operator can tend an entire row of machines.

LOOPING (lower left) Here is the operator at the looping machine. The socks are being finished off at the toe. Some knitted goods must run through several machines before they are completed.

BLEACHING (above) Before silk cloth is dyed it is thoroughly washed and bleached so that the color will be even and have a silky sheen. Here it is being washed and bleached. The long lengths of cloth revolve on two rows of racks above the vats. The cloth gets about two dozen baths before reaching the end where it is removed and taken to the vats in the dye room.

Rayon

When a silkworm eats mulberry leaves a gummy substance is formed in its body from the cellulose in the leaves. The silkworm forces this substance through tiny holes (spinnerets) in its body. Men have learned how to take cellulose from wood and leaves and make a gummy substance by using chemicals. They force it through the tiny holes of a machine called a spinnerette to make rayon threads. **MAKING RAYON YARN** Sheets of cellulose are soaked in a chemical solution (above left) and later shredded into a fluffy pulp. Next the pulp is churned and mixed with a chemical and water until it looks like orange-colored bread crumbs (above, center). Then this material is mixed with more water and caustic soda to form a thick, sirupy liquid called viscose in these great tanks (above, right). The viscose is forced through the many fine holes of the spinnerette into a chemical bath and so becomes filaments (below, left). This spinning machine (below, center) draws the filaments out of the bath and spins them into thread, which is wound onto cones (below, right) for storage and shipping.

Photos: E. I. DuPont de Nemours and Company

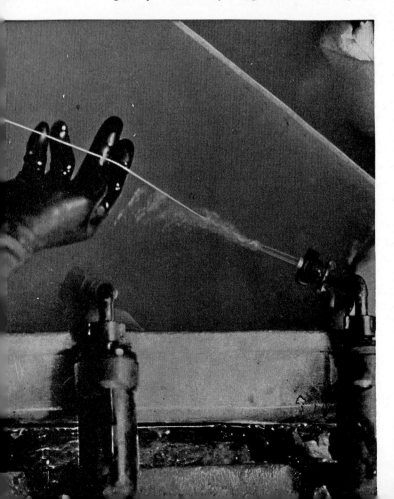

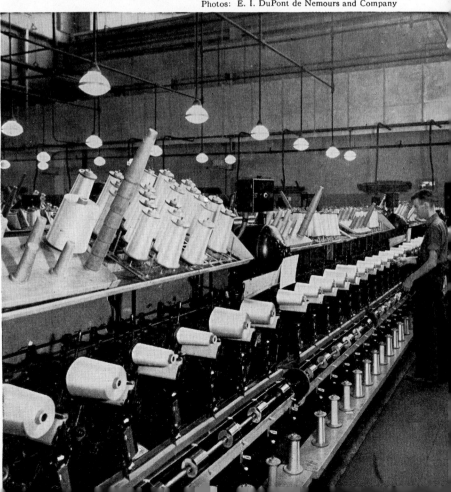

Lumber

In parts of Canada and the United States lumbering is the outstanding occupation. The men who fell the trees and prepare the logs for shipment are called lumberjacks or loggers. They set up camps in the forests, where they live and work during the coldest winter weather.

Perhaps this great spruce tree (left) will be used for violin cases or for railroad ties. Spruce is also used for telegraph and telephone poles, where its strength and durability make it useful. Before sawing a tree, the loggers must plan for it to fall so that it will fall the safest way. After the tree has fallen its trunk is cut into log lengths. Sometimes smooth ice slides make it possible to slide the log down the hillside; again, greased wooden runways are used for this purpose. In more level places, railroads are built into the forests and the logs are pulled by horses or by tractors to the freight cars. In some foreign countries elephants do such hauling. (See page 39.)

A LOG RAFT (below) When the logs reach the river they are taken by water, road, or rail to the sawmills. Sometimes the logs are bound together in a crude raft by a boom or cable. A skilled raftsman can guide a raft over swift currents without losing his foothold. The logs are washed before being taken into the sawmill with the help of a bullchain. After the logs have been cut in the sawmill, they are taken to a planing mill. (See page 40.)

Photos: Monkemeyer Press

A SAWMILL (below) Both circular and band saws are used for cutting logs into lumber in a sawmill. A band saw operated by machinery cut these boards from fir logs. Lever-controlled machinery turns the logs as the planks are cut; they are then ready to be trimmed smooth for marketing.

In the lumber yards the planks are stacked in high layers so arranged that air may circulate between them. Before being used lumber must be dried to remove any remaining sap. The length of time required to dry lumber depends on how wet it is, on the kind of lumber, and on the thickness of the boards. After lumber has been thoroughly dried, or cured, it is ready for the thousands of uses man has for it.

A WOODEN HULL (upper right) Only the strongest and most durable wood should be used in boat building.

A FRAME HOUSE (lower right) This house is built of lumber. Before being used for building, lumber is graded according to its strength, durability, and freedom from knots. There is little waste; even sawdust is sometimes burned as fuel, or when ground to powder and mixed with a glue binder, chalk, clay, and linseed oil, it may be molded into imitation carvings for capitals and ornamental decorations for ceilings. Waste, or scrap wood, may be made into windows and doorsills. Larger scraps may be ground to wood pulp for papermaking.

Photos: Monkemeyer Press (below), Ewing Galloway (upper and lower right)

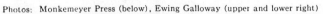

How Paper Is Made

LOGS FOR MAKING WOOD PULP (left) These logs have been cut into handy lengths. They have been put into a revolving drum and all the bark has been removed.

CHIP CONVEYOR (below left) After the logs have been thoroughly washed, they are cut into chips in a chipping machine. This chip conveyor then takes them to the digesters.

THE DIGESTERS (below) These huge tanks are four stories high. In them the wood chips are cooked in acid.

TOP OF DIGESTER (below right) After the chips have been spilled into the digester, the heavy top, which is on the fourth floor, is screwed on tightly. Here the amount of heat, cooking acid, and steam pressure are regulated.

BOTTOM OF DIGESTER (lower right) On the first floor, where the bottom of the digester is located, is the blowoff valve. When the chips are cooked, it is opened. The pressure inside the digester shoots out the soft-cooked chips, blowing them apart into the fibers from which paper is made.

Photos: West Virginia Pulp and Paper Co.; Weyerhaeuser Timber Co.

BLEACHING (left) In the bleaching machine, the top of which is shown here, the wood pulp is bleached (made white) in a solution of chlorine and hypochlorite.

FILTER AND WASHER (right) To free the wood pulp of chemicals, it is washed. Then it passes through some screens to remove knots, cinders, and other matter.

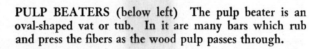

PULP BEATERS (below left) The pulp beater is an oval-shaped vat or tub. In it are many bars which rub and press the fibers as the wood pulp passes through.

JORDAN MACHINES (below right) As the wood pulp passes through these machines, the pulp fibers are carefully brushed and then cut into the proper lengths.

Photos: West Virginia Pulp and Paper Co.

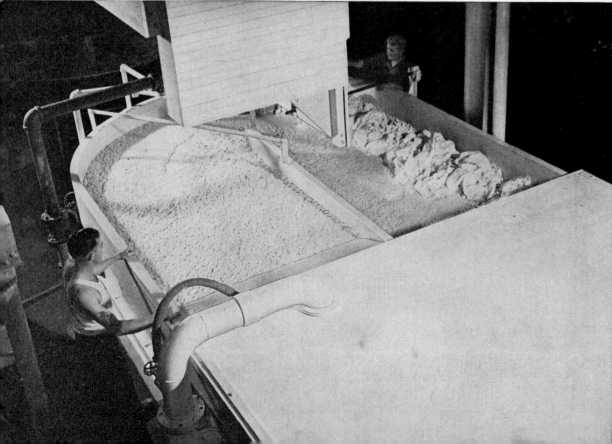

PAPER-MAKING MACHINE (below) This is the "wet end" of a paper-making machine which may be as long as 300 feet. It is made up of a wire-cloth belt on which the fibers are allowed to mat, or to felt, into the form of a sheet of paper familiar to you.

The sheet which has thus formed in the wet end of the huge machine is then passed along between some heavy rollers (right) to squeeze out as much surplus water as possible at this stage.

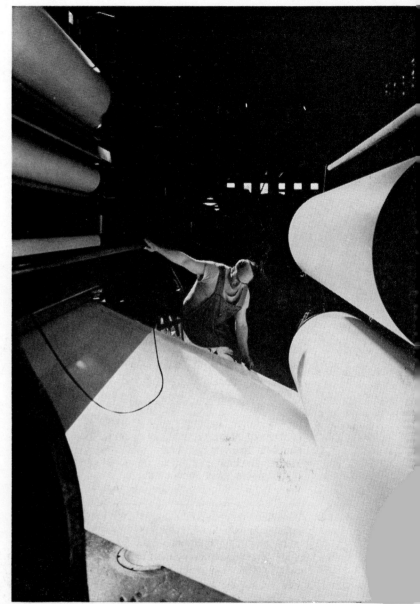

Photos: West Virginia Pulp and Paper Co.

DRYING THE PAPER (left) The sheet is dried by passing it over a number of suction boxes. These drain out most of the water which remains in the sheet.

Before the paper comes out at the "dry end" of the machine (above), it is passed over a number of drier steam-heated cylinders. Then it is cut and wound into huge rolls. The paper is now ready to be shipped to printers and to manufacturers of paper products.

Photos: Armstrong Cork Company

Cork

The cork oak tree (above) is an evergreen growing in Southern Europe and along the North African Coast. It grows twenty to sixty feet high and lives 300 to 400 years. In July and August bark is stripped from its trunk with a long-handled hatchet, incisions being made around its base and immediately under the main branches (upper center). When the trees are between twelve and twenty years old the first stripping is done. The uninjured inner layer forms cork for later strippings, which are made every nine or ten years. The first and second barkings yield a coarse, uneven, inferior grade of cork. With each stripping, however, the quality improves, and the tree thrives under the operations. To make it soft, bark is boiled in vats and scraped to remove the hard covering (right). In flat slabs it is loaded on burros or mules and then taken by railroad to the seaports (lower center). Cork is light, elastic, and waterproof. It is used in making corks, life preservers, linoleum, and other articles of everyday use.

Rubber

LATEX FOR RUBBER (upper left) Each day a worker cuts a small strip of the outer bark of the rubber tree so that a sticky, milky fluid, called latex, may trickle out and be caught. If the bark is carefully and not too deeply cut, it will heal over. The next year the other side of the tree can be tapped. Latex is not the sap of the tree, but comes from the inner bark. Two rubber trees, if tapped for an entire year, will yield about enough rubber for a six-ply tire.

The Indians called this tree caoutchouc, or "weeping tree," because its "tears" flow so easily. An Englishman named the product gum rubber when he found that it would rub out pencil marks.

CULTIVATING RUBBER TREES (lower left) At first all latex came from wild trees growing in jungles of Central and South America, but now trees that produce the most quantity and best quality of latex are grown on plantations in warm countries. When the seeds of a rubber tree are ripe, the pod bursts with a loud snap and the seeds fall to the ground. These are carefully planted and tended. The seedlings must grow for seven years before the trees can be tapped for latex.

Photos: Goodyear Tire & Rubber Company (below, center, and right)

RAW RUBBER (center) Pure rubber is separated from the rest of the latex before being shipped. This is done either by adding chemicals or by allowing the latex to dry out, leaving only the rubber. Here raw rubber is being rolled into huge sheets by machinery at the plantation. These sheets are hung to dry until ready to be packed for shipment (lower center).

SYNTHETIC RUBBER (below) This must be milled to remove moisture before being rolled in sheets similar to those made of raw rubber.

Photos: Ewing Galloway (above); Goodyear Tire & Rubber Company (below)

90

UNPACKING RUBBER (below)   The sheets of rubber at the plantations are folded and tightly pressed into bales or boxes. Raw rubber is so sticky and soft that when it is opened at the factory it is like a solid bale. Note the rollers to the right; these make it easy for the workmen to move the heavy bale to the place of the next operation.

Photos: Goodyear Tire & Rubber Company

PIE-CUTTER (above)   The bales of crude rubber are first taken to a machine called a pie-cutter where they are pressed against the knives of the machine by a hydraulic ram and cut into small chunks. These small chunks of pure rubber are then mixed with other ingredients to make the familiar rubber products of everyday use.   The making of a tire is shown on pages 91 to 93.

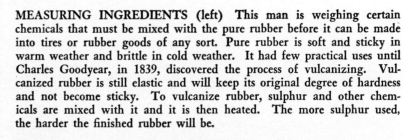

MEASURING INGREDIENTS (left) This man is weighing certain chemicals that must be mixed with the pure rubber before it can be made into tires or rubber goods of any sort. Pure rubber is soft and sticky in warm weather and brittle in cold weather. It had few practical uses until Charles Goodyear, in 1839, discovered the process of vulcanizing. Vulcanized rubber is still elastic and will keep its original degree of hardness and not become sticky. To vulcanize rubber, sulphur and other chemicals are mixed with it and it is then heated. The more sulphur used, the harder the finished rubber will be.

MIXING A BATCH OF RUBBER (below) Here the chemical compounds are being mixed with the pure rubber on the cylinders in a rubber-tire factory. The chemicals and the rubber are rolled between two cylinders until they are worked together thoroughly.

Photos: Goodyear Tire & Rubber Company

BIAS CUTTER (below) The rubberized cloth is cut into bias strips. Behind the workman is the cutting arm of the machine, ready to cut a strip from the calendered rubber and cloth as it hangs like a curtain. These bias strips are called plies, and several of them are put into each tire. It is for this reason such expressions as four-ply and six-ply tires are used in describing tires.

Photos: Goodyear Tire & Rubber Company

A CALENDER (above) This machine is used in making tires. Strong cotton cloth is calendered, or finished with rubber, by a process of rolling. The fabric and the rubber must be of just the right temperatures to unite as they are pressed between these rollers. The fabric makes the rubber tire wear much longer.

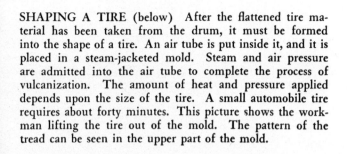

SHAPING A TIRE (below) After the flattened tire material has been taken from the drum, it must be formed into the shape of a tire. An air tube is put inside it, and it is placed in a steam-jacketed mold. Steam and air pressure are admitted into the air tube to complete the process of vulcanization. The amount of heat and pressure applied depends upon the size of the tire. A small automobile tire requires about forty minutes. This picture shows the workman lifting the tire out of the mold. The pattern of the tread can be seen in the upper part of the mold.

Photos: Goodyear Tire & Rubber Company

BUILDING A TIRE (above) This man is building up a tire on a drumhead. Lightweight tires have as few as four plies; giant truck and tractor tires may have as many as thirty-six plies. As the workman puts the bias strips on the tire-making machine he places them so that the threads of the fabric run at right angles to each other. This helps to make the tire extremely strong. After he puts on two or more plies he adds cord fabric which protects the tire from the rim. He then covers these layers with the **rubber sidewall and tread**, unlocks the drum, and removes the flat tire.

Photo: Field Museum of Natural History

Coal

FOREST OF THE COAL AGE (above) About three hundred million years ago the world's first great land vegetation covered the areas where today are found coal deposits. The forests consisted entirely of flowerless, seedless plants: gigantic horsetails and rushes, conifers, ferns, and fernlike plants. Tremendous pressure of the earth overlying these forgotten forests produced the coal.

HEAD OF A COAL MINE (below) At the left is the tipple apparatus that dumps, or "tips," the coal from loaded mine cars into carriers that take it to the mine head. At the right is a cone tank storing 125,000 gallons of water. The water circulates from this reservoir through the wash boxes, into which newly-mined coal is dumped. Impurities in the coal fall to the bottom, the coal is floated onto sorting screens, and from them drops into the row of gondola cars below.

IN A COAL MINE (right) A guide is showing some visitors through a mine. He is pointing out the trunk of a petrified tree in the coal bed. Visitors wear coats to protect their clothing, miners' caps with electric lamps on them, and rubber boots. Much underground water seeps into mines and must be pumped out. Some mines are on or near the surface; others, like this one, extend thousands of feet underground.

Photos: Peabody Coal (below); Lehigh Navigation Coal Company (right)

DRILLING FOR BLASTING (left) These two miners are drilling a hole so that explosives may be put in and the coal blasted loose. Drills are run by electrically-driven machines.

BLASTING (above) A cartridge of compressed air is inserted in the hole. When the air is suddenly released, an explosion occurs which is strong enough to break down the coal.

LOADING MACHINE (lower left) The coal is loaded on to a shuttle car with the help of a power-driven machine. Then the coal is taken to the shaft and hoisted to the surface.

AT THE PITHEAD (below) a mine locomotive takes the coal cars to the spot where the coal is loaded into railroad cars and transported to various parts of the country.

Photos: United States Steel; Peabody Coal Co.; Bituminous Coal Institute

HAND-SORTING (above) Inside the tipple the big lumps from the mine travel along a moving platform while skilled sorters (on the right) pick out slate and rock; other men (on the left) break up the large lumps, preparing the coal for washing and sizing.

PROCESSING (right) In the wash boxes fast-rushing water carries the coal along, but allows the heavier rock and slate to fall to the bottom. Water mixed with air bubbles races through the wash boxes at the rate of 4,000 gallons a minute from the cone tank at the head of the mine (page 94). After it is washed, the coal is run through a rinsing spray. This washes off fine particles of coal that have adhered to the larger pieces. When the coal has been thoroughly dried, it is screened for shipment.

SCREENING (below) Here coal is going over screens. The first screen lets the 1½-inch pieces fall through; the next screen lets the 2-inch pieces fall through; the next, the 3-inch pieces; and so on. The sorted coal is stored into bins or carried away in the gondola cars waiting for it below.

Photos: Peabody Coal Company

Steel

OPEN HEARTH (left) Steel is made by heating iron with other materials which will remove some of the carbon from the iron. Here molten pig iron is being poured into an open hearth furnace. The ladle is carried by a traveling crane and tipped by a hook-and-pulley operated from above.

LADLE (below, left) The ladle of white-hot steel is ready to be picked up by the hooks and poured into molds. Steel workers cannot go near the hot metal but operate pulleys and crane from platforms above.

MOLDS OF MOLTEN STEEL (below, right) The hot metal glows and the sparks shower as the molds are filled. The solid pieces of steel are called ingots. These are sent to rolling mills where they are reheated and pressed into sheets or rolled and drawn into rails.

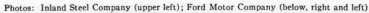

Photos: Inland Steel Company (upper left); Ford Motor Company (below, right and left)

STEEL BRIDGE (right) Steel framework is used for all modern big bridges and skyscrapers. Often it is covered with stone or brick. This is a view of the San Francisco-Oakland Bay Bridge. Notice the steel girders and cables.

CABLE (below) A close-up of one of the cables on the Golden Gate Bridge, San Francisco, the largest suspension bridge in the world. Each cable is made up of 27,572 separate steel wires a little thinner than an ordinary lead pencil. The workmen are tightening a band around the cable.

Photos: American Bridge Company (right); Bethlehem Steel Company (below)

AUTOMOBILE CONSTRUCTION Steel can be made to bend, yet it is strong and will not break or wear out easily. Many pieces of sheet steel are stamped out into the shapes of automobile bodies by huge presses. An automobile body (left) made in this way is being lowered on to the chassis. The front end of the car (lower left) is being lowered into place as the body and chassis move forward on the assembly line. To conserve metals such as steel, copper, nickel, and tin, many parts of automobiles are now made of plastics.

ELECTRIC-ARC WELDING (below) When steel parts must be fastened together so that they will be as strong as a single piece, an electric arc is often used. The word arc refers to the curved "flame," or brilliant flow of current, between the two electrodes. The heat of the arc melts the metals so that they will unite, or weld.

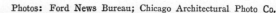

Photos: Ford News Bureau; Chicago Architectural Photo Co.

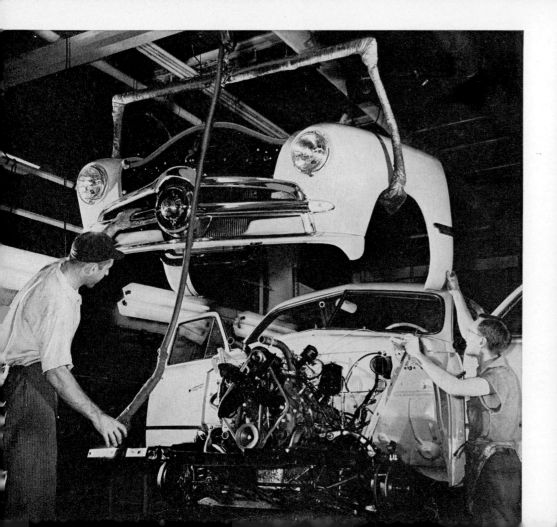

LOCOMOTIVES (right) In order to go faster than the old iron ones, modern locomotives must be lighter and stronger. Steel plates, welded together, make the body.

AN ELECTROMAGNET (below, left) To move great masses of steel, men use an electromagnet. It moves heavy loads as easily as this small electromagnet picks up nails. It is much more powerful than an ordinary magnet, for an electric current runs through it and sets up a strong magnetic field.

ASSEMBLING ARMATURES FOR GENERATORS (below, center) Another use of steel in an automobile factory. The armature is the winding in which electro-motive force is produced. The generator produces current to operate lights and self-starter, and supply the spark to explode the gasoline.

STEEL BUILDING (below, right) Steel girders, the framework of skyscrapers and all large structures, must be fastened together by welding (see page 99) or by riveting. Red-hot rivets are forced into holes in the girder with a riveting machine. When the rivets cool, they contract, thus holding the girders firmly in place.

Photos: Museum of Science and Industry (below, left); Ford Motor Company (below, center)

Photos: Baldwin Locomotive Works (above); Carnegie-Illinois Steel Corporation (below)

Photos: Bethlehem Steel Company (above); Douglas Aircraft Company (below)

Photo: LIFE Magazine

"QUEEN MARY" IN DRY DOCK (above) This shows the stern end of the ship. The framework of the hull is steel. Steel plates are riveted to form the outer covering. The propellers are made of manganese bronze.

STEEL BARGE (above, left) Here a covered barge built entirely of steel is being launched. This barge will be used to carry merchandise on the Ohio and Mississippi Rivers.

AIRPLANE (below, left) To make huge airplanes men must have a metal that is extremely light and yet very strong. Duralumin, an alloy of aluminum, copper, manganese, and magnesium, almost as strong as steel although weighing only one-third as much, is used chiefly in large airplanes; some trains, elevators, and machinery parts are also made of it. In constructing airplanes, exhausts, stacks, collector rings, diaphragms, and heating boilers are frequently made of stainless steel.

Petroleum

Petroleum is a liquid mineral, believed to have been formed by earth pressure on decomposed animal and vegetable matter. Oil is sometimes found near the surface of the ground; often it is deep underground and usually near gas and salt water. The gas can be piped and used for heating and cooking. When the gas is above the oil, its pressure causes the oil to rise in the well and flow out.

OIL FIELD IN TEXAS (below) Wells like these produce crude oil, or petroleum, from which are made gasoline, lubricating and fuel oils, and other products. Derricks are built in order to drill the wells, which may be as much as three miles deep. Generally oil must be pumped, as shown here, where the oil is flowing through the net-work of pipes, pumped by a central power plant, which will handle the flow from sixteen wells.

OIL WELL IN THE GULF OF MEXICO (right) Drilling for oil underwater is a difficult task. This well is one mile out and one mile deep, and was drilled under fourteen feet of water.

Photos: The Pure Oil Company

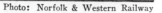

Photo: Norfolk & Western Railway

TRANSPORTING OIL After petroleum is taken from the ground, it is shipped to the refineries. Methods of transporting include: by tank cars (above, right); and by ocean-going tankers (above, left); and also by pipe lines (below, center), through which oil is pumped for hundreds of miles.

REFINERY IN OKLAHOMA (below, left) The largest natural gasoline manufacturing plant in the world. Here gasoline is obtained from crude oil near the field before shipping. Valuable petroleum products are kerosene, motor oils, asphalt, greases, waxes, carbon black, naphthas, and alcohols.

STORAGE TANKS (lower right) So many oil products are liquid that they must be stored in tanks, which may hold 150,000 to 160,000 barrels, and are filled by complex systems of pipe and pumping lines.

Photos: Phillips Petroleum (below, left and center)

Photo: The Pure Oil Company

104

Cement

Builders use cement to bind sand and gravel together into concrete, a building material as hard as rock. Our great dams, as well as many hundreds of thousands of miles of highways, are made possible by the use of cement. It is used also in skyscrapers, factories, and bridges. Three different minerals are needed for making Portland cement. They are lime, silica, and alumina. A formula for making cement includes about twelve parts of lime, five parts of silica, and one part of alumina. The lime is obtained from limestone, cement rock, marl, and oyster shells. Silica is found in shale, clay, cement rock, and the clinkers, or slag, from blast furnaces. Alumina comes from shale, clay, and slag.

GIANT POWER SHOVEL (upper left) This shovel can lift rocks as big as a piano. It loads the cement rock into dump cars. These cars take the rock to the cement plant, where it is crushed.

THE CRUSHING MILL (upper right) The big crusher grinds huge pieces of rock into stones about the size of a hen's egg, just as a coffee mill grinds coffee beans into fine grains. The workman uses a long rod to keep the rocks from clogging in the hopper. His safety belt is attached to chains overhead.

THE BALL MILL (lower left) The small pieces of rock are battered and crushed by metal balls in this grinding machine. Finally the rock becomes a fine gray powder.

THE CEMENT KILN (lower right) This is really a huge furnace, where the powdered cement is roasted, or "burned." A roaring fire heats the cement to 2700° Fahrenheit, more than twelve times hotter than boiling water. The cement glows in beautiful colors and takes the form of marble-sized balls, or clinker. The clinker is ground to powder finer than the finest bread flour, and the cement is ready for use.

Photos: Portland Cement Co.

GRAND COULEE DAM (upper right) This dam is one of the largest structures ever built by man. It contains 50,000 carloads of concrete, laid over a steel foundation. The use of concrete has given man the power to tame the widest, deepest, and swiftest rivers. This dam provides water to irrigate farm lands. Its huge generators make electricity.

CONCRETE MIXER (upper left) Whenever large amounts of concrete are needed, the mixer is put to work. It has automatic devices for measuring the ingredients and mixing them better than can be done by hand.

LAYING A CONCRETE ROAD (lower left) Even though the concrete mixer is hard at work, it takes many skilled workers to construct a cross-country highway; diggers, bosses, engineers, as well as the layers of concrete, all share in the work. Soon it will be hard, dry, and smooth, and ready for trucks and automobiles to pass over it.

Pottery

Clay is found in many places and is used for various purposes, chief among which are the making of bricks and pottery. Clay consists of an earthy substance formed by decomposition of certain rocks with a mixture of various minerals.

A CLAY BANK (right) When taken from the banks clay is prepared for use by processes of cleaning, grinding, and straining. Bits of iron are removed by magnets. When ready for use it is mixed and squeezed through machines called pugmills. Special kinds of pottery are earthenware, stoneware, china, and porcelain.

Photos: Ewing Galloway

CLAY MINE (left) Clay is obtained from mines as well as clay banks. The process by which it is brought from the mine is called tunnel mining. The finest pottery or porcelain is made from a pure white clay called kaolin, meaning "high hill," from a hill in China from which deposits were first taken. Today the United States mines about half the kaolin used for pottery.

Pottery products have been made since earliest times. Nearly all primitive peoples have used pottery vessels for cooking. Some of the most beautiful relics of the ancient peoples of Egypt, Greece, and Rome are pieces of pottery. From them can be learned much of the habits of these peoples; how they stored their wines, oil, and water; and often their grains and other foods were stored in earthenware jars.

A JIGGER (upper left) A revolving mold on which moist clay is placed to fashion plates. The plate is pressed face down on a mold while the undersurface is molded by a form laid over the clay. Pottery vessels may be made by hand, in molds, or by both methods. The potter with moist hands shapes the clay on the wheel as it revolves. He regulates its speed according to his need.

CASTING (below) Some pottery is shaped in molds made of plaster of Paris, and this process is called casting. The molds are made in sections for easier separation. The mold is filled with a thin mixture of clay. As the plaster of Paris absorbs the water, the remaining clay hardens, forming a thin coating upon the inside of the mold. Any watery clay in the center is then poured out.

GLAZING (lower left) Glaze gives gloss to pottery. It is obtained by covering the article with a mixture consisting of lead, lead oxide, boric acid, feldspar, flint, and white clay ground to a fine powder and mixed with water. This mixture is called "slip," and is about the consistency of thick cream. Color effects are obtained by adding various chemicals to this mixture. Glazes are usually added after the first firing.

Photos: Lenox

Clay hardened in drying rooms absorbs moisture again when exposed to damp air. To harden clay permanently it must be subjected to high temperatures for varying degrees of time, usually from thirty-six to forty-two hours. This is done in a kiln in cylindrical earthen vessels called saggers.

SAGGERS (right) These are placed one upon another in a kiln. Before being removed from the kiln, pottery must cool. All clay objects hardened by subjection to heat are called ceramics.

After the first firing, the clay is hard but porous and will not hold water. It is also brittle and easily broken. For greater permanence as well as for beauty it is usually glazed and put through a second firing, much hotter than the first.

A TUNNEL KILN (below) Clay ware passes through this kiln on moving cars. Formerly most pottery was fired in what was called a beehive kiln, filled with saggers stacked around the sides, with the roaring fires built in the center. Glazed pottery requires about three days of heat, sometimes rising as high as 2000° Fahrenheit. The degree of heat depends on the colors or the grade of pottery being made.

Photos: Ewing Galloway

Photos: Pittsburgh Plate Glass Company

Glass

MINING FOR GLASS MATERIAL (above) A sand mine in operation in Missouri, from which silica sand is being taken; sometimes it is dug from an open pit. Glass is made by heating and fusing silica (sand is an impure form of silica) with soda, limestone, and other raw materials. Silica is found almost everywhere.

MEASURING SAND FOR GLASS (upper right) The man rests his wheelbarrow on the scale and watches the hand of the scale as the last bit trickles in. All the ingredients must be accurately measured so that the glass will come out just right. The mask is worn to prevent harmful silica dust getting into the man's lungs.

MELTING TANK (lower right) The ingredients are pushed into the tank and heated to around 3000° Fahrenheit, when bubbling, white-hot molten glass is drawn off. The tank holds about 1,500 tons.

Photo: Ewing Galloway (left); Corning Glass Works (above)

CASTING MOLTEN GLASS (left) Putting glass into molds for railway signal lenses. A ladleful of glowing, molten glass is poured into the mold; the glass, now much like taffy, is cut off. Then the mold is pressed down and the glass cooled.

GLASS BLOWER (above) A man gathers a lump of the proper size on the end of a hollow rod and hands it to the blower. By skillful blowing, swinging, and rapid twisting, the blower can shape the glass as he wishes. The tank contains molten glass; if the lump becomes too cold, it is reheated at the "glory holes" on the side.

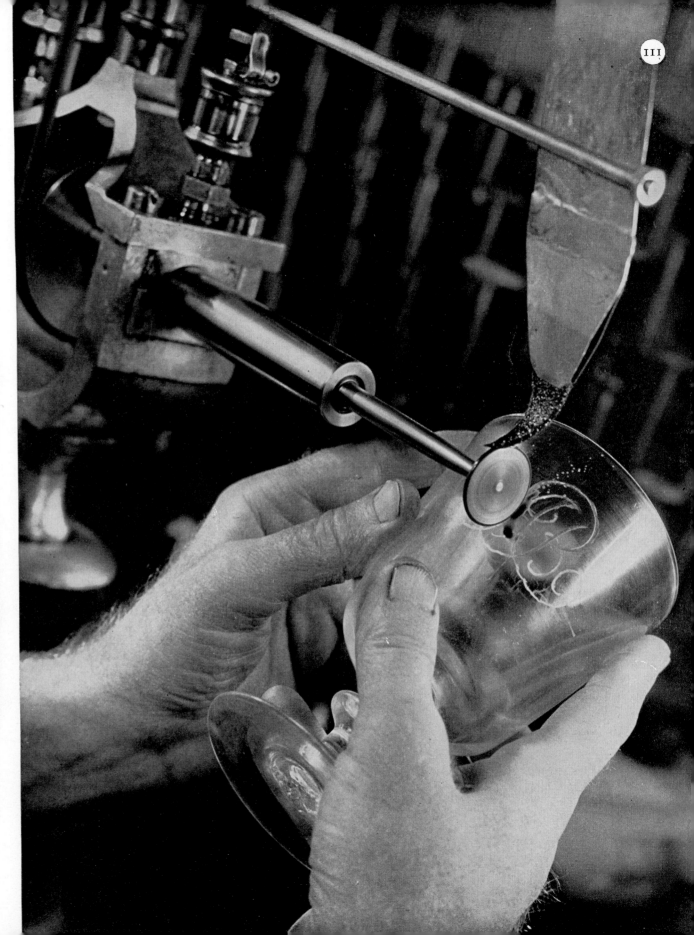

Photos: Corning Glass Works

SHAPING A GOBLET (above) While glass is still soft, it may be cut with shears. After glass has been annealed and hardened, the edge can be ground smooth.

ENGRAVING ON GLASS (right) The artist first draws a monogram on the goblet, then he cuts into the glass with a rotating copper wheel or a diamond point. Some glass is pressed into molds that make designs in it; but pressed glass is never so sparkling as cut glass. Modern American glass is so free of impurities that even ten-cent store ware is clearer than handmade glass of bygone years.

Photos: Kaufmann & Fabry Co.; Morton Salt Co.

Photos: Freeport Sulphur Company

SALT Most of the table salt which we use is produced in evaporating plants (above left) from brine pumped to the surface from salt deposits below ground. Salt is also harvested (top above) in Utah after it has evaporated in the sun. It is also mined (above) in such states as Kansas and Texas.

SULPHUR (above) Wells are drilled (left) to the sulphur formation underground. Superheated water is piped down to melt the sulphur. The melted sulphur is forced up through another section of the same pipe. It cools and solidifies in storage "mountains" (right) from which it is shipped.

COPPER (below) The picture (left) shows a California mine with shafts extending deep into the ground. Most copper ores contain sulphur and rock; after the ore is crushed the rocks are sorted and smelted to remove the sulphur. What remains is smelted again, and the copper is almost pure enough to use. The converters (right) are pouring molten copper into a ladle.

Photos: Anaconda Copper Mining Company

ASBESTOS (below) A fibrous mineral found in serpentine rock. The miner is separating the fibers from the rock with a cobbing hammer (left). The longer fibers are spun into yarn for making asbestos textiles; here rope to pack the joints in furnaces is being woven (right). The shorter fibers are matted, or felted. Asbestos is chiefly used to resist acids, flames, and intense heat.

Photos: Johns-Manville

Photos: Kingsport Press (except lower right)

Printing

TYPESETTING (above, left) Here the typewritten manuscript is being set on a linotype machine, which casts in metal a full line at a time. The operator sits at a keyboard much like one on a typewriter.

ELECTROTYPING (left, center) After type has been set and the pictures reproduced on metal, an impression of them is made on a wax mold, prepared with graphite. By an electric process, a thin sheet of copper is attached to the wax mold. Backed up with lead.

this thin sheet of copper becomes the surface that does the printing.

MAKEREADY (right, center) The electrotype is laid on the bed of the press and carefully checked to be sure every letter hits the press evenly. Flat sheets of paper will be fed onto the large roll of this machine and run over the type, which has been covered with ink by the small roller in the foreground.

BINDING The printed pages must be folded (above, right) before they can be stitched and bound. The machines fold sixteen pages at once. After all the sections of sixteen pages each have been

gathered, the operator sews them along the back edges (below, left). After the rough edges have been trimmed away, the binding is glued on. The glued books (center) are stacked, a heavy weight is laid on top of them; they then stand until they are dry. These pictures are of CHILDCRAFT being printed and bound.

NEWSPAPER PRINTING (below, right) A huge roll of paper is fed on a rotary press and printed from type molded on paper mats. All the work must be done much more rapidly than in book printing. As the papers come from the machine they are folded.

Photo: Chicago Tribune

Transportation

After goods are made in a factory or mill, they must be carried to the persons who want to buy them. The carrying of goods or of people is called transportation. At this moment, a cargo plane may be rushing medicine to miners in Alaska, a boatload of new automobiles may be headed for South America, and a team of oxen may be trudging toward a Chinese city with a cartload of precious rice. In all parts of the world the wheels of transportation are turning. The transportation industry carries goods to us by land, by water, and through the air.

FREIGHT TRAIN (upper left) This puffing locomotive is pulling cars loaded with iron ore for the blast furnaces of a steel mill.

CARGO PLANE (upper right) Air transport is the swiftest way to carry goods great distances. Here, oranges are loaded into a plane.

FREIGHT YARDS (lower left) Here the railroads bring supplies to a great city, and carry away the products of the city's factories. At seaports, trains may transfer their loads to ships (lower middle).

CROSS-COUNTRY TRAILER-TRUCK (lower right) By day and by night, huge trucks rumble over the highways with their loads.

Photos: Ewing Galloway; Sievers from Black Star; Post-Dispatch from Black Star

CARGO-PASSENGER SHIP (upper left) This ship carries goods and passengers between New York City and various ports of South America. Cables attached to the tall white booms lift freight high in the air and then lower it to the storage space, or hold, inside the ship. There are air-conditioned cabins for passengers.

LUXURY LINER (upper right) Big ships such as this one carry passengers across the Atlantic Ocean in comfort.

RIVER SHIPPING (lower left) A towboat on the Ohio River pushes twelve barges, loaded with oil. Broad rivers such as the Ohio and Mississippi are busy highways of commerce.

CANAL BOATS (lower middle) These boats have just gone through a lock on the New York State Barge Canal. The canal carries freight between Great Lakes ports and cities in New York.

LAKE FREIGHTER (lower right) The Great Lakes provide a convenient means of shipping iron ore and grain to industrial centers.

Photos: Grace Line; United States Lines; Ewing Galloway

Telephone

The telephone is the most widely used means of communication. It plays an important part in our family life and in business. By telephone, we can arrange to meet a friend or call the grocer to deliver food to our homes. The telephone even helps us listen to our favorite radio programs, for telephone wires carry the broadcasts of the great radio networks from one city to another. Many thousands of telephone calls are made every minute in the United States alone. Telephone wires cross the continent in all directions, and underwater cables carry calls across the oceans.

SWITCHBOARD FOR SPECIAL CALLS (upper left) These telephone girls answer your call when you wish to speak to the operator. They also put through emergency calls, such as those to the police.

HAND-OPERATED SWITCHBOARD (upper right) This operator completes calls for persons who do not have dial telephones. When she is asked for a number, she plugs in a wire to make the connection.

TELEPHONE CABLE (lower left) Millions of miles of wires are necessary to carry telephone calls. Most of these wires are in underground cables such as this one. The men are splicing the cable.

OVERHEAD WIRES (lower right) Some telephone wires are still carried on poles. All the wires require constant care and checking.

Photos: A.T. & T.; Ewing Galloway

Telegraph

The telegraph was the first high-speed means of communication. Before the telegraph was invented, messages usually could travel no faster than a horseman could carry them. Sometimes it took days for the news of a great event to travel across the country. The telegraph sends messages with the speed of electricity, which is about 10,000 miles a second. Thousands of personal and business messages travel by telegraph each day. One of the most important uses of the telegraph is for dispatching trains. Some telegraph messages are carried by cables laid on the bottom of the sea.

SENDING AND RECEIVING MESSAGES (upper left) The operator in the foreground operates a receiver, which types the message on a tape as keys are pressed in another telegraph office. The girl at her left is typing a message. Electrical impulses cause the same letters to be typed on a receiving tape in some distant city.

TELEGRAMS BY PHONE (upper right) Persons telephone their messages to these operators, who type them for sending.

MULTIPLEX TERMINAL (lower left) The Multiplex system permits the sending of as many as 288 telegrams over one pair of wires at the same time. Each message has a different tone, or frequency, and each receiver picks up only the message to which it is tuned.

RADIO BEAM TELEGRAPH TOWERS (lower middle) These towers relay telegrams by means of very short radio waves, called microwaves.

TELEFAX (lower right) This machine makes exact copies, or facsimiles, of written matter or drawings sent by telegraph.

Photos: Western Union

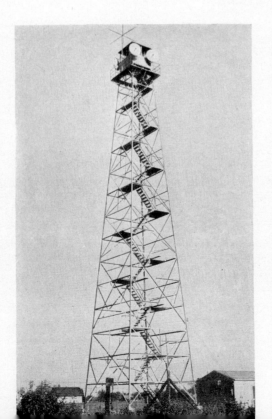

Motion Pictures

THE STUDIOS (below) These are spread over many acres of ground, because often whole villages, sections of large cities, as well as the interiors of huge buildings must be reproduced for the taking of a picture. Many of the largest studios are in California, because it is bright and sunny during most of the year; on dark days or when interiors are taken, the powerful Klieg lights supply illumination that rivals sunlight.

Photos: Paramount

CAMERA AND MICROPHONE (above) An amazing amount of equipment is necessary to film even the simplest type of scene, such as this meeting of two actors. The white square and oval reflectors help the lights to illuminate both sides of the actors' faces and figures. The sound equipment hangs down from the long metal arm. The photographer has a complicated camera, which he can point in any direction.

Radio

Radio plays an important part in our lives. It brings the greatest works of music and drama into our homes. It helps the farmer by giving weather forecasts, market prices, and other useful information. The police use radio to help them protect lives and property.

REHEARSING A PROGRAM (upper left) The announcer at the microphone is rehearsing his script. The engineer in the foreground controls the loudness, or volume, of the voice. At his left is a machine for making recordings.

THE TRANSMITTER (upper middle) usually is located in the country, where there is no electrical interference to cause static.

A STUDIO PROGRAM (upper right) George is thinking over a difficult question.

MASTER CONTROL BOARD (lower right) Here a constant check is made to assure radio listeners of clear, uninterrupted programs.

Photos: A. J. Mills from F.P.G.; N.B.C.; WGN

PICTURES BY RADIO (above) A young radio actress shows us a picture of herself which has been transmitted by radio. This kind of picture transmission is called facsimile. The process has been used to send photographs, maps, and diagrams across continents and oceans in a matter of seconds.

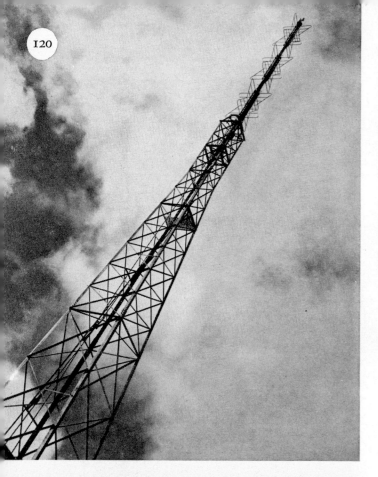

Television

Television uses radio waves to send both pictures and sounds through the air. By means of television, you can watch a ball game, a play, or the inauguration of a President without leaving your living room. Television also has many other uses. It permits a surgeon to demonstrate a new kind of operation to hundreds of doctors and students at one time. It is used to send maps and charts from ship to plane or from one office to another.

TELEVISION ANTENNA (upper left) A single antenna sends both the sound and the picture signals of television. The television programs sent over this transmitter can be seen and heard for forty miles in any direction. Beyond that distance, the programs must be relayed, or picked up and sent on by a RELAY STATION (upper right).

CONTROL ROOM (upper middle) Here the television engineers keep a careful check on the transmission of the program, to make sure that pictures and sound are clear.

TELEVISION PROGRAMS are of two kinds. One is the on-the-spot telecast of a public event, such as a baseball game (lower left). The other is the studio show (lower right).

Photos: R.C.A.; N.B.C.; A.T. & T.